MEROE

A Civilization
of the Sudan

Meroe, a civilization that arose on the banks of the Nile in what is now the northern part of the Republic of the Sudan in the eighth century B.C., played a vital role in the cultural development of the African continent. But its rich heritage of architecture, sculpture, and artistic objects had been largely forgotten until recently, when research and excavation brought the remarkable achievements of the Meroitic people to light.

"The comparative lack of interest in the area," explains Professor Shinnie, "arises partly from its geographical remoteness and partly from a mistaken view that Meroe was a mere provincial and barbarous copy of Pharaonic Egypt." It is Professor Shinnie's aim "to show ... that Meroe was a power in its time, had a distinctive culture of its own, and that it may have contributed to the spread of techniques and ideas in the African continent."

P. L. Shinnie reconstructs the history of the period from the sites and artifacts found in excavation, and offers a provisional assessment of the mysterious and still largely undeciphered Meroitic language. The author has culled the works of classical authors to show that the civilization of Meroe was well known throughout the Roman Empire and remained of some importance at least until the end of the second century A.D. He surveys the great explorations, from the late eighteenth century to those engendered by the building of the Aswan Dam.

Supplemented with numerous photographs and drawings, MEROE is a graphic view of a people in close contact not only with the rest of the continent but with key spheres of influence ranging from the Roman Empire to Persia.

Ancient Peoples and Places

MEROE

General Editor

DR. GLYN DANIEL

ABOUT THE AUTHOR

Peter Shinnie was Professor of Archaeology at the University of Ghana from 1958 to 1966 and is now Professor of Archaeology at the University of Khartoum. He was field director of the University of Ghana's excavations at Debeira West until early 1966, a project which was part of the UNESCO-sponsored campaign to save the Nubian monuments from the rising waters behind the Aswan Dam.

Ancient Peoples and Places

MEROE

A CIVILIZATION
OF THE SUDAN

P. L. Shinnie

84 PHOTOGRAPHS
57 LINE DRAWINGS
6 MAPS

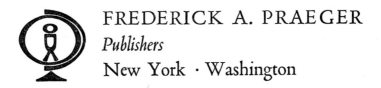

FREDERICK A. PRAEGER
Publishers
New York · Washington

THIS IS VOLUME FIFTY-FIVE IN THE SERIES

Ancient Peoples and Places

GENERAL EDITOR: DR. GLYN DANIEL

BOOKS THAT MATTER

*Published in the United States of America
in 1967 by Frederick A. Praeger, Inc.,
Publishers, 111, Fourth Avenue,
New York 10003, N.Y.*
All rights reserved
© *Peter Shinnie 1967*
Library of Congress Catalog Card Number: 66-125118 ?
Printed in Holland   66-25118

DT
73
M4
35

CONTENTS

LIST OF ILLUSTRATIONS   7

PREFACE   12

I   THE DISCOVERY OF MEROE   13

II THE RULERS AND THEIR
    CHRONOLOGY   29

    CHRONOLOGICAL TABLE   58

III TOWNS, TEMPLES AND CEMETERIES 62

IV ART   99
    General   99
    Sculpture   101
    Pottery   114
    Jewellery and personal adornment 122
    Metalware   126
    Glass   130

V   LANGUAGE   132

VI RELIGION AND BURIAL CUSTOMS   141
    Burial customs   146

126872

VII THE PEOPLE AND THEIR LIFE:
    MEROE AND AFRICA   153
        Physical appearance   154
        Domestic buildings   156
        Furniture   157
        Agriculture   158
        Iron-working   160
        Tools and weapons   162
        Meroe and Africa   165

    NOTES ON THE TEXT   170

    BIBLIOGRAPHY   184

    SOURCES OF ILLUSTRATIONS   184

    THE PLATES   185

    NOTES ON THE PLATES   217

    INDEX   224

ILLUSTRATIONS

PLATES

1 Pyramid N. 22 at Meroe
2 The Meroe pyramids
3 Temple of Amun, Meroe
4 Kiosk, Meroe
5 The Sun Temple, Meroe
6 The Sun Temple, Meroe
7 The Palace, Wad ben Naqa
8 The Lion Temple, Naqa
9 The Palace, Wad ben Naqa
10, 11 The Lion Temple, Naqa
12 The Lion-god, Naqa
13, 14 The Kiosk, Naqa
15 Temple F, Naqa
16 Granite ram, Naqa
17 Musawwarat es-Sofra
18 Central temple, Musawwarat es-Sofra
19 North-east temple, Musawwarat es-Sofra
20 Musawwarat es-Sofra
21 Statue fragment, Meroe
22 Column drum, Musawwarat es-Sofra
23 Statue, Argo Island
24 Statue from Temple of Isis, Meroe
25 Statue from royal bath, Meroe

PLATES 26, 27 Pair of statues, Meroe
        28 Bronze head of Augustus
    29, 30 Gold figurine of a queen, Jebel Barkal
        31 Slate plaque with king and Lion-god, Meroe
        32 Stone stela of a king, Meroe
        33 Sandstone plaque of Prince Arikankharer, Meroe
    34, 35 Bronze statuette of a king, Kawa
        36 Bronze head with cartouche of Arnekha-mani, Kawa
        37 Sandstone head of *Ba* statue, Faras
        38 Hellenistic bronze head, Meroe
     39–41 Painted pots, Faras
        42 Painted and incised pot, Faras
        43 Painted and impressed pots, Faras
     44–59 Pottery, Faras
        60 Gold jewellery, Meroe
        61 Gold rings, Meroe
        62 Gold amulets, Meroe
        63 Necklaces, Faras
64, 65, 67 Bronze bowls, Meroe and Faras
        66 Bronze bowl, Gemai
        68 Bronze bottle, Faras
     69–73 Bronze lamps, Meroe and Faras
        74 Silver porringer, Meroe
    75, 76 Bronze mirror cover, Faras
        77 Bronze hanging vase, Faras
     78–81 Silver goblet, Meroe
     82–84 Glass vessels, Meroe and Faras

8

FIGURES

1   Map of Nile Valley, p. 14

2   Map of Meroitic Kingdom, p. 17

3   Engraved scene on bronze bowl from Karanog, pp. 18, 19

4   Latin inscription from Musawwarat es-Sofra, p. 23

5   Cartouche of Queen Amanishakhete, p. 49

6   King Amanikhabale's name on bronze cone from Kawa, p. 49

7   Rock carving of King Sherkarer at Jebel Qeili, p. 51

8   Map of the Island of Meroe, p. 53

9   Axumite inscription from Meroe, p. 57

10 Map of Faras, p. 64

11 Types of graves at Faras, p. 65

12 Plan of Western Palace, Faras, p. 66

13 Plan of Amara East temple, p. 67

14 Plan of the temples at Kawa, p. 68

15 Reliefs on temple B, Kawa, p. 69

16 Map of Napata area, p. 71

17 Section through pyramid and burial chamber, p. 72

18 Plan of Jebel Barkal temples, p. 73

19 Map of Meroe town, p. 76

20 Plan of Amun Temple, Meroe, p. 78

21 Plan of Sun Temple, Meroe, p. 82

22 Sun Temple relief, Meroe, p. 83

23 Plan of the temples at Naqa, p. 88

24 Pylons of Lion Temple, Naqa, pp. 90, 91

FIGURES   25   Head of god, Lion Temple, Naqa, p. 92
           26   Plan of Musawwarat es-Sofra, p. 93
           27   King riding elephant, Musawwarat es-Sofra,
                p. 95
           28   Relief from pyramid chapel of Arqamani, Meroe,
                p. 107
           29   Reliefs from pyramid chapel of Nahirqa, Meroe,
                p. 109
           30   Restored reliefs from Lion Temple, Musawwarat
                es-Sofra, p. 110
           31   Thumb rings on hands of king and god, Musaw-
                warat es-Sofra, p. 111
           32   Thumb ring, p. 111
           33   Lion-god with body of snake, Naqa, p. 112
           34   Lion-god's standard, p. 112
        35, 36 Offering tables, p. 113
        37-41   Pottery types, pp. 114, 115, 116, 118, 119
           42   Painted patterns on pottery, p. 121
           43   Gold plaques from Meroe, p. 123
           44   Gold earrings, p. 124
           45   Gold and silver rings, p. 124
           46   Silver plaques of lion and lion's head, p. 125
           47   Faience amulets, p. 125
           48   Elephant from a bronze bowl, Meroe, p. 127
           49   Emblem and inscription on bronze lamp, p. 128
           50   Engraving of a cow from a bronze bell, Meroe, p.
                129
           51   Burial at West Cemetery, Meroe, p. 147
           52   Burial at West Cemetery, Meroe, p. 149

FIGURES
53 *Stelae from Karanog, p. 151*
54 *Pottery coffin from Argin, p. 155*
55 *Plan of house at Gaminarti, p. 157*
56 *Folding stool, p. 158*
57 *Pots on* saqia *wheel, p. 160*
58 *Metal rod for painting eyes with antimony, p. 162*
59 *Iron shears, p. 163*
60 *Sword wielded by King Netekamani, p. 163*
61 *Iron spearheads from Meroe, p. 164*
62 *Bronze quiver, p. 164*
63 *Iron arrowhead, p. 165*

Preface

MY INTEREST IN MEROE was first aroused, when, a newcomer to the Sudan, I was taken there in 1947 by my friend A. J. Arkell, at that time also my chief. Even as recently as that, few had heard of the place and fewer were interested in it. Now its name is frequently on the lips of the ever growing number of scholars concerned with the history of Africa, and once more active research in the field of Meroitic studies proceeds.

So often is Meroe mentioned and so little is it known, that a book to summarize the present state of knowledge seemed desirable; and though this book has been too long in the writing there has been some advantage in this, since each of the last five or six years has produced important additions to our understanding of Meroitic history and culture.

It does not pretend to be comprehensive. The limitations of size mean that much has been left out and many detailed arguments treated only summarily. But I have tried to give a general view of what we now know of a fascinating and important part of Africa at a crucial moment in its history.

My indebtedness to others will be manifest in the references, and I cannot mention them all. But I owe a special debt of gratitude to A. J. Arkell, who first instructed me in the archaeology of the Sudan. I have also benefited much from discussions with other colleagues, J. Leclant, J. Vercoutter, F. Hintze and W. Y. Adams being foremost amongst them; Dows Dunham, the doyen of Meroitic studies, has likewise given me much help and I am indebted to him for supplying many of the illustrations. Finally, I must thank my wife who has helped at every stage of this book, and done many of the drawings as well as participating in all my field work.

P.L.S.

CHAPTER I

The Discovery of Meroe

THE CIVILIZATION of the ancient state of Meroe has long remained the least known of those of the ancient world. Although it flourished from the sixth century BC to the beginning of the fourth century AD in southern Egypt and the northern Sudan, it was virtually forgotten and unstudied until recent times.

The comparative lack of interest in the area (a recent book on the history of the outskirts of the Roman Empire dismisses it in one brief sentence)[1] arises partly from its geographical remoteness, which has meant that, until very recent times, few have devoted themselves to the study of the period and area; and partly from a mistaken view that Meroe was a mere provincial and barbarous copy of Pharaonic Egypt, and that it contributed nothing to the world and had no importance in world development. It is the aim of this book to show that this view is wrong, that Meroe was a power in its time, had a distinctive culture of its own, and that it may have contributed to the spread of techniques and ideas in the African continent.

It was well known to the classical world. Herodotus was the first ancient writer to mention Meroe by name, although earlier writers from Homer onwards had known in general terms of the Ethiopians, the 'burnt faces', a term closely paralleled by the Arabic use of the word Sudan (from *Beled es Sudan*, 'the country of the Blacks') to describe the same area today. Herodotus, whose description of the world in his time was published in about the year 430 BC, devoted one complete book to the Nile Valley. He visited Egypt and during the course of this journey went as far south as the town of Elephantine, the modern Aswan, which he describes as being at the frontier between Egypt and Ethiopia, by which he meant the Meroitic state.

Fig. 1

Fig. 2

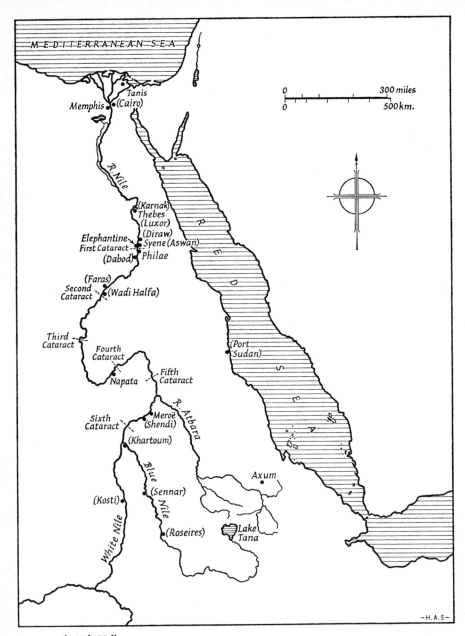

Fig. 1.   *The Nile Valley*

This was as far south as he went; but he must certainly have met Meroites at Aswan and there can be little doubt that much of his information was gained from them. His geographical information is incomplete but in outline it is reasonably accurate. He describes the winding river Nile, and he was certainly properly informed about the Fourth Cataract where, he tells us, it is necessary to land and to travel forty days along the river bank, since rocks in the river make boat travel impossible. This timing of the journey along the non-navigable stretch is too long, but slight exaggeration by a Meroite anxious to make his homeland safe from foreign interference might easily have led to a statement of this sort. The twelve days by boat beyond the cataract before reaching Meroe, which he calls the capital of the 'other Ethiopians', is slightly exaggerated but not unreasonable.

Herodotus then goes on to tell us that by going up-stream for the same length of time as that taken by the journey from Elephantine to Meroe, one came to the country of the deserters, the 'Asmach', so called, he says, because they stood on the left of the king. These were Egyptians who had deserted from the army of the Pharaoh Psammetichus II during his campaign in the Sudan in 591 BC. Many attempts have been made to identify the area where these deserters settled, one of the more recent suggestions being that they went far up the White Nile and settled in southern Kordofan not far from the Bahr el Ghazal.[2]

In Book III Herodotus describes the activities of the Persian King Cambyses who, he tells us, sent spies to see if the 'Table of the Sun' was in the land of Ethiopia. If such spies were in fact sent, it was probably for the purpose of spying out the land for a future military expedition. Herodotus tells us that the Table was said to be in a meadow on the outskirts of the town of Meroe and that this meadow was always full of meat, being replenished by the magistrates every night so that whoever came there might eat of it during the day. Whatever the truth of this story, it is certain that worship of the sun was one of the cults of Meroe, and Garstang in his excavations found a temple some little way from the town, in what might well be called the out⁄ skirts, which he assumed to have been dedicated to the worship of the sun.[3]

The remainder of the information that Herodotus gives is of a somewhat mythological nature. He tells us how Cambyses' spies went to the Ethiopian king with various gifts, a purple robe, a gold necklace, a jar of wine, and other things, but that the king of Meroe was not deceived. Instead, he stressed how powerful his country was, and gave the spies a bow which he said the Persian king could try to draw though he doubted if he would succeed. He told them of the long life of his people who were said to live for 120 years owing to their diet of boiled meat and milk. They were shown the 'Table of the Sun' and other wonders and then returned to their Persian master. On their return, Cambyses set out with his army to invade Ethiopia but found the harshness of the country such that he turned back before he ever reached the capital.

There is no further mention of Meroe for nearly 400 years until Diodorus Siculus, who (Book I, section 32 ff.) describes the course of the river Nile, tells us that it has its source in Ethiopia, and that it passes through a number of rocky cataracts. The Nile, he adds, has various islands including that known as Meroe, and states strangely that the city of that name was founded by Cambyses. The description of Meroe as an island is not an uncommon one; it is, in fact, nothing of the sort, but it does lie in an area which is surrounded on three sides by rivers, and this region was often referred to as the 'Island of Meroe'.

The whole of Book III deals with Ethiopia, as classical writers called the area of the modern Sudan; it is not very useful to our purpose, but does describe the ritual murder of the king of Meroe by the priests. Diodorus tells us that the practice came

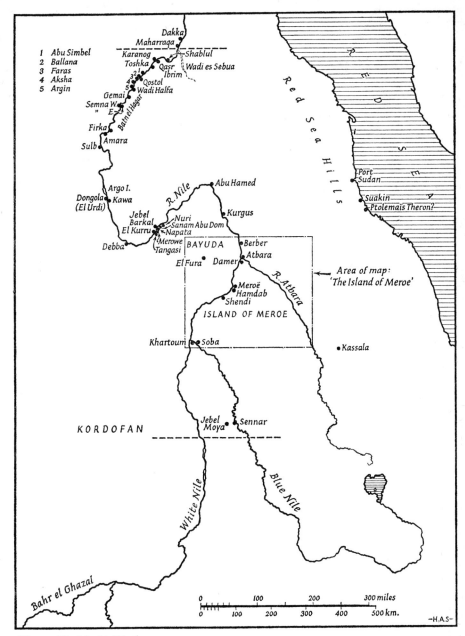

1 Abu Simbel
2 Ballana
3 Faras
4 Aksha
5 Argin

Dakka
Maharraqa
Karanog   Shablul
Toshka   Wadi es Sebua
        Qasr
        Ibrim
        Qostol
        Wadi Halfa
Gemai
Semna W.
      " E
Firka
Sulb   Amara
Batn el Hagar

Argo I.
Dongola   Kawa
(El Urdi)
        Jebel
        Barkal   Nuri
        El Kurru   Sanam Abu Dom
                   Napata
Debba   Merowe
         Tangasi   BAYUDA   Berber
              El Fura   Damer   Atbara
                        Meroë
                        Hamdab
                        Shendi
              ISLAND OF MEROE

Khartoum   Soba   Kassala

KORDOFAN

        Jebel
        Moya   Sennar

R. Nile

Abu Hamed

Kurgus

R. Atbara

Red Sea Hills

RED SEA

Port Sudan
Suakin
Ptolemaïs Theron?

← Area of map:
'The Island of Meroe'

White Nile

Blue Nile

Bahr el Ghazal

0   100   200   300 miles
0   100   200   300   400   500 km.

—H.A.S—

Fig. 2.   The Meroitic Kingdom

Fig. 3.   Rural scene engraved on a bronze bowl from Karanog. Length of decoration 11.2 cm.

to an end in the reign of King Ergamenes, a contemporary of Ptolemy II of Egypt; Ergamenes, who, he says, had a tincture of Greek learning and some knowledge of philosophy, brought his troops into the temple and killed the priests. It has been suggested that Ergamenes had been educated by Greeks in Egypt but there is no warrant for this in the text itself. It seems more likely that he owed his education to some of the wander-ing Greek scholars who must have passed up the Nile to try their fortune in this strange and little known town of the far south.

The next writer to give us information of importance was Strabo. He wrote a *Geography* in about 7 BC and collected in-formation on Egypt and Ethiopia during the years 25 to 19 BC, when he was in Egypt. He tells us that he went as far south as Philae, just beyond Syene (Aswan), with his friend Aelius Gallus, the Roman governor.

He is mainly concerned with geographical description which is in many ways very accurate. He, like Diodorus, also calls Meroe an island, and correctly describes it as being above, that is to say up-river of, the place where the Astaboras (the Atbara) flows into the Nile. He also speaks of the confluence of the Nile and the Astasobas which must refer to the junction of the Blue and White Niles at Khartoum, some 120 miles further south.

Strabo also gives a number of other details of interest. He says there is no rain at Meroe. This is not quite accurate, for a

certain amount falls there nearly every year, though a little way
to the north rain is very scarce. He gives us many details of the
life of the people, telling us that they lived on millet from which
they also made a drink; this is still so, the drink being the local
beer, known in Sudan Arabic today as *marisa*. Most of them,
we read, were poor nomads wandering from place to place
with their flocks – as is still true of many peoples of the Butana[4].
He also reports that there were no fruit trees except the date
palm, and gives many other details of fair accuracy. The
deserters are also mentioned by Strabo, and are said to be at a
place called Tenessis, which cannot be identified; and once
again Cambyses is regarded as important at Meroe, since it is
he who is said to have given the town its name. The most important information about Meroe from Strabo is his account of
the war between Meroe and the Romans during the tenure of
office of Gaius Petronius as Roman prefect of Egypt (25 to
21 BC). Details of this will be found below where the history
of Meroe is discussed, but it is worth noting that, in the description of the events of the campaign Strabo tells us that the commander of the Meroitic army was a general of Candace, a name
known to us from other ancient writings and for a long time
interpreted as a proper name. We now know from a study of
the Meroitic sources that it was not a name but a title whose
meaning is not absolutely clear, but is perhaps something like
'Queen Mother', or 'Queen'. It is written in Meroitic in a
number of places, of which the most relevant is in an inscrip-

tion from Kawa which gives the name of Amanirenas followed by the title Candace. It is possible that she was the queen reigning at the time of the Roman invasion. The Greek writer Dio Cassius briefly mentions this campaign and also speaks of the Meroitic leader as Candace.

Pliny in his *Natural History* (VI. 35) also writes of Meroe and gives another account of the campaign of Petronius, as well as some geographical description and a list of towns, most of which are unidentifiable and which he tells us no longer existed in his day. His evidence, he says was the report of a group of Praetorian troops which had been sent to Ethiopia by the Emperor Nero in about AD 61.

The story of this expedition is of very great interest. We do not know the size of the party, but it was under the command of a Tribune, so it is unlikely to have been a very small one. Pliny describes the route to Meroe, and, a real note of authenticity, says that the troops reported that round Meroe itself greener vegetation begins, some forest comes into view, and tracks of rhinoceros and elephant are to be seen. Greener vegetation does in fact begin once the area of annual rain is reached and Meroe lies within this region. There is no longer a forest there but there are plenty of trees, and before the depredations of man in recent times, it is certain that the whole area was far more wooded. Elephant and rhinoceros are no longer to be seen, but there is no reason why they should not have been present. Representations of elephants in Meroitic art are sufficiently common for it to be certain that they must have been a familiar sight. Pliny also states that the town of Meroe is seventy miles from the first approach to the island, which presumably means from the crossing of the river Atbara, and this is reasonably accurate. There was, he says, a temple of Amun in the town, and he tells us that Meroe was ruled by a queen, again Candace, a name which he says was passed on to a succession of queens, thus getting nearer the truth than other writers.

The persistence of this tradition that the ruler of Meroe was a queen is curious. It occurs also in the only reference to Meroe in the New Testament, where, in the Acts of the Apostles VIII, 26–39, the story is told of how Philip baptised 'a man of Ethiopia, a eunuch of great authority under Candace queen of the Ethiopians', another indication of how widespread knowledge of Meroe must have been in the first few centuries AD. In spite of this view, widely held in the Roman Empire, we know that the normal ruler was a man, but women played an important part and are frequently shown on the temple and funerary chapel reliefs. This story that Meroe was ruled by a queen must reflect the importance that attached to queens in Meroitic society.

Another account of an expedition to the Sudan is given by Seneca (*Nat. Quest.* VI 8,3) who says that he heard from their own lips the story told by two centurions of the expedition they made at the order of the Emperor Nero to investigate the source of the Nile. They claimed that with assistance and letters of introduction from the king (not this time a queen) they went into the heart of Africa. They came to huge marshes, and the river was so entangled with vegetation that only a one-man boat could pass. This sounds very like a first-hand account of the *Sudd* of the southern Sudan, where vegetation in the river was a major obstacle to all the early explorers. The account also says that these men saw two rocks from which water issued at the source of the Nile, but in spite of much ingenuity these have not been identified.

It has generally been assumed that these two accounts refer to the same expedition and that the Seneca version is more likely to be accurate, since he claims to have heard at first hand from those taking part. In a recent publication, however, Hintze[5] has suggested that two different expeditions are being described, and points out that the members of the two parties are different. Pliny's account has a troop of Praetorian troops under a Tribune, whilst Seneca speaks only of two centurions; secondly, the aims of the expeditions seem to be different – Pliny's was a military reconnaissance, Seneca's to investigate the source of the Nile; and thirdly Seneca describes how, after reaching Meroe, they got the help of a king for their journey southwards, whilst Pliny's tribune found a queen in control.

Though other classical writers refer to Meroe, they add no-thing to our knowledge and make either passing references or give reports which have a purely mythical air. But they do show that the Meroitic state was well known to the Roman Empire, and that it remained of some importance at least until the end of the second century AD. Juvenal mentions it twice; once, to say that the women of Meroe have breasts bigger than their fat babies – presumably an idea derived from the appreciation of fat women which was certainly a feature of Meroitic life well portrayed in temple reliefs; and in another place, to tell us that some superstitious women go to Meroe for lustral water to sprinkle in the temple of Isis at Rome.

Meroe is also referred to in various works of fiction of which the best known is the *Aethiopica* of Heliodorus. This work, written in the third century AD, shows that its author knew of Meroe and he makes the heroine daughter of its king. His local colour, such as it is, does not tell us anything of Meroitic life, but he knew that the physical appearance of the Meroites was different from that of the Egyptians and Persians, and his ac-count of the siege of Syene may preserve a memory of some Meroite attack on that town. He had also heard something of the military tactics of the Meroites and describes their use of lightly armed troglodytes as skirmishers.

That is the extent of our knowledge of Meroe from the clas-sical writers, but it is sufficient to show that although Meroe was geographically remote from the main centres of civilization of the classical world, it was known to that world and that there was coming and going between the Mediterranean and the Upper Nile. We have some records of Meroitic embassies to Rome in graffiti in the Dodecaschoenos[6] as well as the account by Strabo of the mission to Augustus at Samos, sent by the Meroites after their defeat by Petronius. Visitors from the Mediterranean to Meroe have left no account, except perhaps that given to Seneca, and no traces of their visits have been found, although the presence of objects from the Mediterranean in Meroitic burials attests the trade that must have been carried on. Two possible exceptions to this are the column drum from Meroe, now in Liverpool and still unpublished, which has the Greek alphabet written round it, perhaps from a school and witness to an attempt to teach Meroitic children the elements of Greek; and the often quoted inscription from Musawwarat es-Sofra:

Fig. 4

BONA FORTUNA DOMINAE
REGINAE IN MULTOS AN
NOS FELICITER VENIT
E URBE MENSE APR
DIE XV VIDI TACITUS

This is the text as usually published, but many of the readings are far from clear.[7]

After these more or less contemporary accounts of Meroe, knowledge of it faded and no additional information was obtained until European travellers and archaeologists went there in comparatively recent times. The general ignorance of Africa

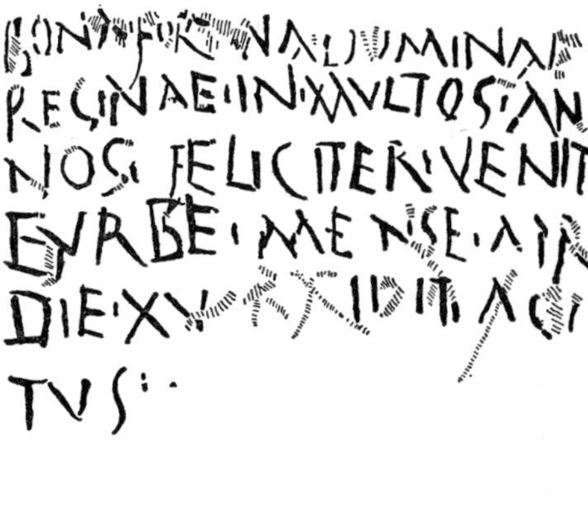

Fig. 4. Latin inscription from Musawwarat es-Sofra (after Hintze)

which persisted until the great explorations of the late eighteenth and the nineteenth century enveloped ancient Meroe as well, and even the site of its capital was forgotten until James Bruce (1730–94) travelled through it in 1722.

Bruce was returning from his two-year stay in Abyssinia[8] by way of the Nile, and had come from Sennar up the Blue Nile where he stayed at the court of the Fung king. His route took him along the Blue Nile and then down the main river below the confluence with the White Nile at the spot where Khartoum now stands. On his journey north from this point along the east bank of the river he passed by the village of Begarawiya and the ruins of Meroe, where he saw 'heaps of broken pedestals and pieces of obelisks' and noted: 'It is impossible to avoid risking a guess that this is the ancient city of Meroe.' Curiously enough he does not seem to have noticed the pyramids, although they are clearly to be seen on a ridge a short way to the east. His assumption that the ruins he saw were those of ancient Meroe was based on his knowledge of the classical writers, but it had to wait over a hundred years for confirmation.

In April 1814, Burckhardt, on his way from Damer to Shendi, passed by but did not realise the significance of the ruins nor, as he explains, did he have any opportunity for investigation. He says,

...We passed low mounds consisting of rubbish and red burnt bricks; they were about eighty paces in length, and extended quite across the arable soil, for at least one mile, eastwards, turning, as I thought, towards their extremity, a little more to the south. The bricks were of very rude make, much coarser than those now in use in Egypt. The mounds have the appearance of having served as a wall, although but little remains by which to form a judgement. Both on the northern and southern side we passed some foundations of buildings, of moderate size, constructed of hewn stones. These were the only remains of antiquity I could discover;

nor could I see any stones scattered amongst the mounds of rubbish, as far at least as my sight could reach. A closer examination might, perhaps, have led to some more interest- ing discoveries, but I was in the company of the caravan, and had the wonders of Thebes been placed on the road, I should not have been able to examine them.[9]

The next visitors to the site who have left any account were those who came to the Sudan with the Turco-Egyptian army sent by the Viceroy of Egypt, Mohammed Ali, under the com- mand of his son Ismail in the year 1820. A number of Euro- peans accompanied this expedition, and of them two French- men were particularly concerned with antiquities and have left us important accounts of the ancient sites that they saw. Of these two men the best known is Cailliaud, who published an account of his journey in 1826.[10]

Unlike Bruce, Cailliaud was deeply interested in archae- ology and came prepared to make a detailed study of all the monuments he could find. He visited Meroe in 1821, where he examined and described the pyramids as well as the town site. He then passed on to the south going as far as Sennar. On his return, he went south-eastwards from Shendi in March and April 1822 to visit Naqa and Musawwarat es-Sofra, at both of which sites he stayed and made his usual careful plans and drawings. The publication of his work in 1826 first drew the attention of the learned world to these previously unknown monuments.

Linant de Bellefonds, who was just ahead of Cailliaud, is less well known. His diary has only recently been published,[11] while most of his excellent plans and drawings are still un- published. He first passed through the ruins of Meroe in No- vember 1821, but did not stop, intending to visit the area again on his return from his visit to Sennar far to the south. He returned on his way north in February 1822, and, basing him- self at Shendi, remained in the district until 2nd April, when he left Begarawiya on his further journey northwards to Egypt. He, like Cailliaud, studied the monuments with some care and made plans and drawings. He went to Musawwarat es-Sofra, thus becoming the first European to visit the site, where he stayed for three days making drawings and plans. He also copied some of the many graffiti on the walls and left a record of his visit inscribed on the west wall of the central temple.[12]

Linant returned to Shendi and a few days later set out for Naqa where he again made drawings. Returning once more to Shendi, he left for the north on the 24th March, and on the next day reached the village of Begarawiya where the town of Meroe stood. He spent most of his time at the pyramids, where he again made an excellent plan and did a number of drawings of the pyramids themselves as well as of some of the reliefs on the funerary chapels attached to them. These drawings by the first two travellers to see them are of very great value in showing us the state of preservation of the monuments at the time, and give a number of valuable details of parts since destroyed.

The next visitor of whom we have any information was the Englishman Hoskins,[13] who travelled in the Sudan in 1833; like Cailliaud and Linant, he was much interested in antiquities and studied and recorded many of the monuments he saw on his journey. He came to Meroe in March 1833, and also visited Musawwarat es-Sofra which he considered to be

... the last architectural efforts of a people whose greatness was passed away, their taste corrupted, and all the lights of knowledge and civilization just extinguished. The elegant pyramids of Meroe differ as widely in taste and execution from the immensely extensive but ill-planned ruins of Wadi al-Awateib, as the best sculpture at Thebes, during the age of Rameses II, differs from the corrupted style under the Ptolemies and Caesars.

From Musawwarat es-Sofra, he visited Wad ben Naqa, but never reached the temples at Naqa since his artist refused to accompany him, being frightened by accounts of the presence of lions, and Hoskins himself seems to have been short of money and time. He therefore returned northwards by crossing the Bayuda desert. On reaching the river again, he went to Jebel Barkal, where he had drawings made of the ruins and also visited the Nuri pyramids.

The interest aroused by these discoveries was considerable and rumours of great treasures to be found in the pyramids caused at least one excavation to be carried out. This was by Ferlini, an Italian doctor of medicine in the Egyptian service, in 1834. Ferlini[14] was convinced that treasure would be found in the pyramids and claimed to have removed the tops of several in his search for treasure and, if we are to believe his account, did find a remarkable haul of jewellery in the pyramid known as N. 6 in the northern cemetery.

In the years 1842 to 1844 the Royal Prussian Expedition led by Lepsius travelled through Egypt and the Sudan, recording meticulously a large number of monuments. Lepsius was a leading scholar of his day and had far greater knowledge of Egyptian history than any of the earlier visitors. He had some idea of the chronology and significance of the civilization he was studying, but it was not until the excavations of Garstang in the town site at Begarawiya that it was finally established that this was certainly the site of the famous Meroe of the classical writers.

Garstang, who worked there from 1910 until 1914, when the first World War put a stop to his labours, excavated on a large scale in the town, as well as at the Sun Temple and the Lion Temple, and in cemeteries in the plain between the town and the sandstone ridge on which the pyramids were built. These, which are the tombs of the royal family of Meroe, were excavated by Reisner between 1920 and 1923. He also excavated the royal pyramids of the earlier rulers at Kurru and Nuri. These have now been published by Dows Dunham.[15] In the years 1907 and 1908, Woolley and MacIver excavated in Egyptian Nubia at Areika and Karanog,[16] the first modern excavations of Meroitic sites, and in 1910–1913 the important site at Faras, where a very large cemetery has provided some evidence for the history of Meroitic pottery, was excavated by Griffith.

During the period between the wars interest in Meroitic archaeology waned although important material for the earlier periods was obtained from the Oxford excavations at Kawa.[17] In the last few years there has been a recrudescence of activity with the excavations at Musawwarat es-Sofra by Hintze, as well as his survey of the Meroitic sites in the Butana[18] and the work of Vercoutter and Thabit Hassan at Wad ben Naqa.[19] More recently the building of the Aswan Dam has engendered considerable archaeological activity in Nubia, which has resulted in the excavation of a number of Meroitic cemeteries and of a few dwelling sites. In 1965 the University of Ghana started new excavations at the town site of Meroe; these are being continued by the University of Khartoum.

From these early accounts and from the excavations of more recent times some picture of the culture of ancient Meroe can be obtained. Unlike Pharaonic Egypt, it cannot yet speak for itself and until the Meroitic language is understood, the work of archaeologists alone will further illuminate this ancient African civilization.

CHAPTER II

The Rulers and Their Chronology

THE ORIGINS of the Meroitic state lie far back in the period of Egyptian occupation, and to understand the influence of Egyptian ideas in all aspects of Meroitic life it is necessary to look at the earlier history.

Egypt ruled with various vicissitudes a large part of what ultimately became Meroitic territory for a period of at least 1,500 years, and first occupied the area effectively in the Middle Kingdom (*c.* 2000–1700 BC) when the famous series of forts through the Second Cataract region were built as frontier defences. This period closed with Egyptian withdrawal, per-haps to meet the menace of Hyksos invasion. With the New Kingdom (*c.* 1580–1100 BC) a new pattern of Egyptian occup-ation began and Egyptian control was exercised over a far greater area, the whole stretch of river as far up-stream as the Fourth Cataract being occupied. Towns and temples were built and an organised Egyptian administration was set up.

Although there are inscriptions of Tuthmosis I at Kurgus[1] up-stream of the Fourth Cataract, it seems clear that this cata-ract marked the frontier of effective occupation, and it was here at its down-stream end that the town of Napata came into existence as an important administrative centre. Near it the hill of Barkal, which stands up out of the flat riverside plain and constitutes a remarkable landmark, became of great religious significance; at least as early as the XIX Dynasty a temple to the god Amun was built at its foot. It was served by a colony of priests who were originally Egyptians, although they may have recruited members of the local population as time went on.

During the New Kingdom, Egyptian influence was strong, and besides administrators and priests, a variety of craftsmen and artists introduced Egyptian methods and art forms. The culture of the area became completely Egyptianized, and archaeologists have as yet discovered no distinctive native material from the period. Even after the political decline of Egypt at the end of the New Kingdom, Egyptian cultural influence remained supreme and the excavations at Sanam Abu Dom, near modern Merowe[2] show that objects of Egyptian style, though made by locally resident Egyptian craftsmen, continued to be common and were found in great numbers in the graves of the eighth century BC.[3]

It was from this highly Egyptianized society that the first native ruling dynasty arose in the period after the withdrawal of Egyptian administration. Before *c.* 750 BC the first Sudanese state of which we have any detailed knowledge developed. This state, with its capital at Napata, was ancestral to that of Meroe, and became for a short time a world power.

Strictly this book is concerned only with the history and culture of the period after the centre of political power had been shifted from Napata to Meroe; but, seeing that many writers use the term Kush or Cush to cover the whole period from the start of the independent state of the end of Meroe,[4] it is necessary to give a sketch of earlier times.

The origins of the rulers of Napata are unknown, but there is no reason to assume that they were not natives of the area, and the view of Reisner[5] that they were of Libyan origin has little to support it. The evidence for their existence is to be found in the cemetery at Kurru on the right bank of the Nile, about nine miles downstream from Jebel Barkal. Here on high ground a short way from the river were some thirty burials, and a relative chronology has been worked out[6] from their location and from the typology of the tomb forms. This suggests that the first burials date from the middle of the ninth century BC.

Of the earliest rulers we have no information, but after Kashta we have virtually a complete series of names. Piankhy and his immediate successors are well known to us from a number of sources written in Egyptian, and they figure in Egyptian history as the XXV Dynasty, having started an invasion of Egypt in the reign of Kashta.

This is not the place to go into the detailed history of the Napatan conquest of Egypt and a convenient summary has been made by Arkell.[7] Here it suffices to say that Piankhy completed the conquest of Egypt and that he and his successors, of whom Taharqa was the most noted, controlled that country until 654 BC, when, as a result of Assyrian campaigns in Egypt, Napatan power there was broken, and Tanwetamani, the last Kushite king of Egypt, retreated to his own land.

All the early kings, with the exception of Taharqa, were buried at Kurru.[8] Taharqa was buried in a new royal cemetery at Nuri on the opposite bank of the river to Kurru and about fourteen miles up stream.

Taharqa's pyramid in this cemetery is the first of a series in which his successors, except for Tanwetamani, were buried, and it is largely on the evidence from these burials[9] that the slender thread of the history and chronology of the time is spun.

The date of the move of the capital of Kush to Meroe and the beginning of the Meroitic phase still remain very obscure. The conventional date as given in earlier books was about 308 BC, but this must be too late, since Herodotus, writing a short while before 430 BC, knew of Meroe and described it, whereas he does not mention Napata at all.

There is little archaeological fact on which to assume a date for this move. It is certain that a town existed at Meroe from early in the sixth century if not earlier. The names of Aspelta, Amtalqa, and Malenaqen, all of whom were buried at Nuri, have been found at Meroe and there were even earlier graves in the South Cemetery there.[10] From the existence of these graves, Reisner argued that from as early as the reign of Piankhy a branch of the royal family had come to Meroe to hold the southern area for the king.

The first king to be buried at Meroe itself was probably Arakakamani who was reigning at the end of the fourth century, but burial elsewhere does not necessarily exclude the possibility of a ruler having lived and reigned at Meroe; we know from a stela at Kawa (No. IX) that Amani-nete-yerike, who was buried at Nuri, lived at Meroe *c.* 431–405 BC according to Hintze or *c.* 435–417 BC according to Dunham.[11]

A sixth-century date seems in many ways to be the most probable one. Wainwright suggests[12] that the story by Diodorus Siculus and others that Cambyses (529–522 BC) was the founder of Meroe grew out of the knowledge that the town was founded at about the time of the supposed invasion by the Persians, that in this way the two become associated, and that this invasion in fact took place.

Perhaps the answer to this problem lies in the discovery that the Egyptian Pharaoh Psammetichus II carried out a campaign in Kush in 591 BC. The evidence for this has been discussed in an article[13] which shows that the well-known Nubian campaign in the third year of this king was of greater importance than had previously been assumed, and that the Egyptian army reached Napata.

A confirmation of this is to be found at Abu Simbel, where the Carian and Greek mercenaries, of whom the army was largely composed, wrote many graffiti on the colossal statues of Rameses II, as well as on the columns of the temple. One of these graffiti, in Greek, gives the names of the leaders of the army, Potasimto and Amasis, and says that they went upstream of Kerkis.

All this indicates an important advance right into the Kushite domain and since Herodotus, writing only about 160 years later, mentions an attack on Napata by Psammetichus' army, it is reasonable to assume that this attack on the capital and its destruction took place. Broken statues of several rulers, of whom Aspelta is the latest, were found at Barkal, and the coincidence of the known date of the campaign with the date of Aspelta suggests very strongly that the destruction occurred as part of the sack of the town and temples of Napata.

If this interpretation of the evidence is right, the damage done to Aspelta's capital would provide a very cogent reason for the move to Meroe which could then be dated to about 591 BC. It is worth noting in support of this view that Aspelta's name is the earliest one known from Meroe, so that in default of more precise evidence we can assume that Meroe was in existence and that the royal residence was transferred there from Napata at the very beginning of the sixth century.

Whatever the precise date of the shift to Meroe, Napata certainly remained of great religious significance at least until the reign of Nastasen (*c.* 385–310 BC), since he and several predecessors had had to travel there from Meroe to be confirmed in their title to the throne by the priests of Amun. Nastasen was the last king to be buried at Nuri and perhaps from about the end of the fourth century BC even the religious importance of Napata had come to an end.

Though political and military events, such as the suggested sack of Napata, may have been amongst the reasons for the shift of power to the south, there can be little doubt that the more favourable economic position of Meroe must have been an extremely important factor.

Meroe stands within the region of annual rain, and the broad valleys of the Butana, the Wadi Awateib and the Wadi Hawad, could produce an abundance of crops and pasture for animals to support an urban civilization which the narrow strip of cultivated land between the desert and the river at Napata could never achieve.[14] It is not only the possibility of increased and easier food production which makes the location of Meroe a favourable one; it is also in a region where there is abundance of iron ore as well as the timber required for its smelting, and, as we shall see, this enabled Meroe, as soon as knowledge of iron-working had been learned, to become a vitally important centre of this new technique.

The town was also well placed for trade, being on a navigable stretch of river at the end of easy caravan routes from the Red Sea. The Nile route to Egypt was not an easy one and was liable to break down in periods of disorder.[15] The series of cataracts made it almost impossible to carry goods the whole way by river, and it was usual to cross the desert from Korosko or the Second Cataract to a point upstream of the Fourth Cataract. This desert crossing could only be maintained when the state was sufficiently strong to preserve the discipline and organization necessary to control and administer the caravans. The breakdown in communications after the expulsion of the XXV Dynasty from Egypt andt he withdrawal to Napata was never fully restored, and expeditions to reopen them, such as perhaps that of Psammetichus II, were not wholly successful. Diodorus Siculus tells us that Ptolemy Philadelphus did partially restore communications but we do not know how far up-river this was effective and it is clear that contacts were few.

Since the Ptolemies and the Romans after them needed the products of Africa, amongst which gold and elephants were important, they had to find another and easier route, and they developed trade down the Red Sea to its African coast. We know of the establishment of Ptolemais Theron especially for the purpose of bringing out elephants, and though the site of this port has not been established, it must be somewhere along the stretch of coast between Port Sudan and the Eritrean frontier.[16]

Meroe is well placed for easy access to the Red Sea, and routes eastwards from the Nile have been in use throughout history. It is likely that these routes were of importance to Meroe, and it is not without significance that two major sites, Naqa and Musawwarat es-Sofra, are at approximately one day's march to the east of the river.

In Roman times, if not earlier, much trade to the Mediterra-
ne an was carried from south Arabia, and even Ethiopia, by the
land route through Arabia to Petra, and there was considerable
contact across the Red Sea between the north-east coast of Africa
and Arabia. Much of the eastern flavour discernible in Meroitic
art and monuments is probably due to this contact, and it is
also likely that some of the Hellenistic and Roman objects
found in royal burials came by way of the kingdoms of south
Arabia.

Very little is known of events from the reign of Aspelta onwards and much of the chronology is speculative. The information on which a chronology and the king list on pp. 58–61 are
based is very scanty. The order and dates of the first six kings
of Kush, from Kashta to Tanwetamani, are reasonably certain
and cross-references are available from Egyptian sources. There-
after three fixed dates have always been assumed: the reign of
Aspelta, known to coincide with the campaign of Psammetichus II in 591 BC; the reign of Arqamani (*c.* 248–220 BC),
who has been thought to have been the Ergamenes of Diodorus
and a contemporary of Ptolemy II (285–246 BC) and of Ptolemy IV (221–205 BC); and Teqerideamani (*c.* AD 246–266),
who is known to have been reigning in AD 253 from the
evidence of a demotic inscription at Philae. However, in recently reviewing the evidence for the date of Arqamani in the
light of his discoveries at Musawwarat es-Sofra, Hintze no
longer regards him as contemporary with Ptolemy II, and
would date him to 218–200 BC.[17] So perhaps all we can say is
that *c.* 220 BC is not far out as a date for this king.

These are the only, even approximately, fixed points in a
history of nearly 900 years. The list of kings is based on names
found in the royal burials at Kurru, Nuri, Barkal and Meroe,
all of which were excavated by Reisner. The order in which
they are placed was worked out by him on the evidence of the
position of the burials in the cemeteries, it being assumed that

the best and most commanding positions were occupied first and that the later burials were arranged further and further away. Further evidence of relative dates has been obtained by a detailed typological study of the pyramids themselves, their style and construction, as well as by study of the objects in them.

From this study, completed and modified by Dunham,[18] it can be seen that the burials fall into a series of quite well-defined groups. The order of the groups has stood the test of later criticism and seems reasonably certain. The order of rulers within them is less certain, but until further evidence is available, must be allowed to stand. Hintze[19] has made some further modifications and his order of kings and suggested dates is given in the table below (pp. 58–61). The dates used in the text are those of the Hintze list.

The dates for the kings as printed give a spurious air of reliability, and it must be made clear that all of them, with the exception of the three kings already mentioned, are pure guesses. The lengths of reigns are assumed from the size of the pyramid and the quantity and quality of the funeral furniture. These criteria, by which the larger pyramids and richer furniture are assumed to be those of kings who reigned longer than those with poorer monuments, may be valid, but the number of years given is no more than an estimate and dates cannot be precise.

All that we can say is that apparently twenty-four kings reigned from 593 to 220 BC, and that it is possible to suggest which ones had long, and which short reigns. This gives an average reign of 15.5 years, a figure not inconsistent with an approximate average reign of fifteen years, which has been suggested elsewhere as normal for African rulers.[20] After Anlamani, a further eighteen kings seem to have been buried at Nuri. Using the average of fifteen years, the eighteenth reign would have ended in 323 BC and this is near enough to Hintze's dates for Nastasen (335–315 BC) to enable us to accept them as a reasonable indication of that king's rule.

Of these eighteen kings, we have detailed knowledge only of three who left inscriptions, Amani-nete-yerike, Harsiotef, and Nastasen – the others are only names. It is possible to see some cultural change during the period and, from Malewiebamani onwards, knowledge of Egyptian hieroglyphs is less, and a lowering of standards of workmanship can be observed.

The inscription of Amani-nete-yerike, which was put up in his honour on the wall of Taharqa's temple at Kawa gives us many details. It is extremely interesting linguistically as well as historically;[21] the language in which it is written is Egyptian, but it shows that knowledge of that language was fading and it was probably no longer spoken. The variations in the quality of the Egyptian in different inscriptions at Kawa – and there are four of this king – indicate that the educational standards of the different scribes must have varied considerably. The great inscription of Amani-nete-yerike (Kawa No. IX) is of funda-mental importance for the history of the period, since it con-tains the first mention of Meroe, and tells us that the king resided there. Inscribed when he was forty-one years old, it first describes a campaign against the *Rehrehs*, who seem to have been occupying the north end of the Island of Meroe. After defeating them, he went to Napata to be accepted as king by the priesthood of Amun, and took part in a ceremony in the Barkal temple where he was recognized in the traditional way by the god. From Napata, he sailed down-stream to an un-identified place called *Krtn,* probably on the right bank, where he fought the *Meded,* a people described as 'desert dwellers'; later he went on a seventeen-day journey from Napata to Kawa and to Pnubs (Argo?), where he gave land to the temple. He then returned to Kawa, where he cleared the approach to Taharqa's temple and ordered repairs to be carried out to a number of buildings. The other inscriptions of this king are extremely obscure in meaning, and add nothing to history, but No. XII gives a regnal year of at least twenty-five (?) for him.

Harsiotef has also left an inscription which gives us some information.[22] It dates from the thirty-fifth year of his reign and is similar in subject matter to that of Amani-nete-yerike, describing the journey to Napata to be accepted by the god, and military campaigns against *Rehrehs* and the *Meded* as well as others. The inscription is written in markedly better Egyptian than that of Amani-nete-yerike and this suggests either that Harsiotef should be placed earlier in the series, or that he was able to employ an Egyptian scribe or, if a native one, one far better educated than those available to his predecessor. Briggs, who examined fragments of human skull from Harsiotef's tomb, assumed them to be of the king and says 'the king was somewhere in his middle twenties when he died'.[23] This is difficult to accept in view of the clear 'year 35' of the inscription, and perhaps the skull fragments were of someone else since there were fragments of at least two bodies in the tomb. Harsiotef's tomb is the first one to contain iron models of tools as well as the usual copper ones, and it is perhaps from this time that the use of iron was beginning to become known at Meroe though, as Wainwright[24] has shown, it was not extensively used until later.[25]

Nastasen was the last king to be buried at Nuri and he, like Harsiotef, left an inscription at Barkal. This[26] closely resembles those of Amani-nete-yerike and Harsiotef in its subject-matter, though it provides extra information of importance and perhaps gives a check on the date of Nastasen. Like his predecessors, Nastasen had to travel from Meroe to Napata to be acclaimed king and he gives us a number of details of his journey across the Bayuda desert which enable us to reconstruct the route.[27] After the ceremony in the temple of Amun the king made the usual royal progress to Kawa, Pnubs and Tare (a place not identified, but also visited by Harsiotef). He campaigned against the traditional enemies and also against an invader who came from the north with a fleet.

The reading of the name of this invader has caused some difficulty. Originally read as *Kmbswdn*, the name was assumed to be that of Cambyses, but this, unless the whole chronology of early Meroitic times is seriously wrong, is impossible, since Cambyses' invasion was *c.* 525 BC. Hintze has re-examined the problem[28] and suggests that the name should read *Hmbswtn*. He argues that this is probably to be taken as a version of the name Khabbash, which is known to us from Egyptian sources,[29] as that of a local ruler in the area between the First and Second Cataracts. Khabbash was fighting in Egypt *c.* 338–336 BC, and if the campaign in Kush took place after that in Egypt, it would have been in about 335 BC. Since Nastasen fought him at the very beginning of his reign, a slight alteration in the original dating given by Reisner (328–308 BC) brings Nastasen's date into conformity with what we know of Khabbash, and may thus provide another fixed point in the chronological framework.

In addition to the main royal cemeteries at Nuri and Meroe, there is also a group of pyramids at Barkal. Typologically they belong to the period just after Nastasen, but no royal names have been found in them and they have been something of a mystery. If their ascription to this period is right – and the archaeological evidence strongly suggests it is – Reisner's idea that they represent the burial places of an independent line of rulers who established a state free of the influence of Meroe and reasserted the importance of Napata may well be correct, although MacAdam[30] has suggested that those buried here were rulers of the whole country.

It is perhaps significant that Nastasen was the last king to be buried at Nuri, and seems to be closely, perhaps immediately, followed by Arakakamani, who was buried in pyramid S. 6 at Meroe. At such a moment there is nothing improbable in a split in the Kushite state. Several royal names, not otherwise known, occur at Kawa; they are approximately of this period, and it is tempting to see in them the rulers of an independent kingdom of Napata who were buried at Barkal.

Plate 36

Until recently the name of Arnekhamani was known only from Kawa where it occurs on a bronze bust.[31] Reisner assumed that he was buried in tomb Barkal 11 and had ruled the whole state until about 300 BC when the southern area became in-dependent under King Arakakamani, who had his capital at Meroe.

Arnekhamani's name is now known, however, from Musaw-warat es-Sofra, and this makes it virtually certain that he also ruled at Meroe. From the writing of his name on the Lion Temple and its resemblance to Ptolemaic royal titles, it seems clear that he was roughly contemporary with Ptolemy IV (221–205 BC), and Hintze would now date him to *c*. 235–218, would include him in the main list of rulers, and suggests that he was buried at Meroe in pyramid N. 53. This change necessitates a considerable revision of the order of rulers and of their dates at this time,[32] as can best be seen by comparing the two lists of rulers given in the table, remembering that Dunham's list was drawn up before the discovery of Arnekhamani's name in the Island of Meroe.

We have no information about Arakakamani to help in the reconstruction of the history other than that he was the first king to be buried at Meroe. His successor, Amanislo, left his name on two granite lions, usually known as the Prudhoe lions, which, originally made in the reign of the Egyptian king Amen-ophis III (1405–1370 BC) for his temple at Sulb, were moved to Barkal perhaps by Amanislo himself.[33] The occurrence at Barkal of the name of a king known to be buried at Meroe must cause some doubt, if the dates are right, as to the exist-ence of the suggested independent Napatan state. These two kings together with Queen Bartare are the only rulers to be buried in the South Cemetery at Meroe. After the death of Bartare, the pyramids were built along a ridge running north and form what is known as the North Cemetery, the main royal burial ground at Meroe.

One of the earliest of the kings to be buried in this new cemetery, and the only one about whom we have any information from outside sources was Arqamani. He built part of a temple at Philae and part of another at Dakka, and this suggests that Meroitic power now reached as far as the First Cataract. Other parts of the same temples were built by Ptolemy IV and there may have been an alliance between them, although since Ptolemy V defaced Arqamani's names at Philae, this perhaps did not last very long.

Arqamani has usually been assumed to be the Ergamenes who is mentioned by Diodorus Siculus. Diodorus tells us that King Ergamenes had some Greek learning and that he killed the priests of the temple of Amun, presumably at Napata, in the reign of Ptolemy II (285–246 BC). The assumption that Arqamani was contemporary with Ptolemies II and IV has caused him to be dated to *c.* 248–220 BC, although in fact it could only be said with any certainty that his reign fell between 285 and 205 BC. Hintze's new proposals for dating, caused by the need to insert Arnekhamani into the king list and to give him a date contemporary with Ptolemy IV, makes it necessary to reconsider the dating of Arqamani and his identification with Ergamenes. If Hintze's dating and order of kings is approximately right, Arqamani cannot have been a contemporary of Ptolemy II, and it may be that the king of whom Diodorus writes was Arakakamani, whose name would not have to be much distorted to give Ergamenes as a Greek version. A rather later date for Arqamani certainly makes it easier to understand the joint Meroitic and Egyptian building activity in Lower Nubia. On the old dating an overlap of only two years between Ptolemy IV and Arqamani does not allow much time for the buildings to have been put up, and it does not seem probable that Ptolemy would have been able to devote resources to

work in the south before his victory at the battle of Raphia in
217 BC, and the conjunction of his name at Dakka with that
of Arsinoe to whom he was only married in the same year is a
further argument that Arqamani was reigning later than 220
BC. The closer contact with Egypt may well be the cause of the
improved quality in the reliefs of Arqamani's pyramid chapel,
which are in good Egyptian style.[34]

An impoverishment of building is shown after pyramid
N. 20, probably that of Tanyidamani (*c.* 120–100 BC), where
the normal custom of a three-roomed burial chamber was for
the first time abandoned, all subsequent tombs being of only
two rooms. Since from about this time we have inscriptions of
Ptolemy VII (145–116 BC) and Ptolemy VIII (111–80 BC) on
the temple at Dabod, we can surmise that political power must
have weakened, and that much of the area down-stream of
Faras was in Egyptian hands.

Another group of pyramids at Jebel Barkal seems on typological grounds to belong to the first century AD. Only Queen
Naldamak's name is to be found there, and there are no other
inscriptions to permit the identification of the buried persons,
but from about the same period there are a number of names of
rulers on the monuments whose burial places are uncertain.

Reisner suggested another line of rulers independent of Meroe
and called it the Second Meroitic dynasty of Napata. Hintze
has followed him, whilst revising the dates, and suggested the
following list of rulers at Napata:

Naldamak	60–44 BC	Bar. 6
Teriteqas	44–26 BC	Bar. 2
Amanirenas	26–18 BC	Bar. 4
Akinidad	18–3 BC	Bar. 9
A Queen	3 BC–AD 12	Bar. 10

Dunham, while agreeing that some of these rulers were probably buried at Barkal, includes their names in the main list. He

also suggests that Teriteqas was buried in pyramid N. 21 at Meroe.

This, or any other, reconstruction must be regarded as completely hypothetical and all we can say is that during this period there were a number of rulers for whom it is difficult to find pyramids at Meroe, except perhaps N. 21, and that there are contemporary pyramids at Barkal whose occupants are not named.

In view of the geographical distribution of the royal names at this period there must be considerable doubt as to the existence of a separate state at Napata. A King Tanyidamani, whose name is known from the Amun temple at Meroe, also left a stela at Napata,[35] which suggests that he controlled that town; and the names of Amanirenas and Akinidad, are found not only in the north at Dakka and Kawa, but also at Meroe itself.[36] Teriteqas also has his name at Meroe, as well as having it associated with Amanirenas and Akinidad at Dakka. So, of the five rulers who it is suggested may have ruled from Napata, the names of three have been found at Meroe.

The dating of these rulers largely depends on the interpretation of the large inscription of Akinidad from Meroe, which has been taken to be an account of the campaign against the Romans which ended with the victory of Petronius in 23 BC.[37] If Dunham's dates for Akinidad are approximately right, then the inscription cannot refer to these events, but until we know more about the Meroitic language, we cannot go further. There is other evidence that Amanirenas and her son Akinidad were the opponents of the Romans,[38] and that therefore Amanirenas should be identified with the Queen Candace of the Latin accounts.

Hintze has made an attempt to reconstruct the history of the period and suggests that it was the Napatan kingdom that fought the Romans, and certainly Strabo's account assumes that the capital was at Napata. Hintze would see Teriteqas as husband of Amanirenas, with Akinidad as their son and crown prince, and thinks that all three went to Dakka, where they left their names on the temple, to campaign against the Romans. Teriteqas died soon after and Akinidad led the campaign.

Our only information about this campaign comes from the classical writers, referred to in Chapter I. The fullest account is by Strabo,[39] who says:

Now Aegypt was generally inclined to peace from the outset, because of the self-sufficiency of the country, and of the difficulty of invasion by outsiders, being protected on the north by a harbourless coast, and by the Aegyptian sea, and on the east and west by the desert mountains of Libya and Arabia, as I have said; and the remaining parts, those towards the south, are inhabited by Troglodytes, Blemmyes, Nubae, and Megabari, those Aethiopians who live above Syene. These are nomads, and not numerous, or warlike either, though they were thought to be so by the ancients, because often, like brigands, they would attack defenceless persons. As for those Aethiopians who extend towards the south of Meroe, they are not numerous either, nor do they collect in one mass, inasmuch as they inhabit a long, narrow and winding stretch of river-land, such as I have described before; neither are they well equipped for warfare or for any other kind of life. And now, too, the whole of the country is similarly disposed to peace. And the following is a sign of the fact; the country is sufficiently guarded by the Romans with only three cohorts, and even these are not complete, and when the Aethiopians dared to make an attack upon them, they imperilled their own country. The remaining Roman forces in Aegypt are hardly as large as these, nor have the Romans used them collectively even once; for neither are the Aegyptians themselves warriors, although they are very numerous, nor are the surrounding tribes. Cornelius Gallus, the first man appointed praefect of the country by Caesar, attacked Heroonpolis, which had revolted, and took it with only a few soldiers, and in only a short time broke up a sedition which had taken place in the Thebais on account of the Tributes. And at a later time Petronius, when all that countless multitude of Alexandrians rushed to attack him with a throwing of stones, held out against them with merely his own body-guard, and after killing some of them put a stop to the rest. And I have already stated how Aelius Gallus, when he invaded Arabia with a part of the guard stationed in Aegypt, discovered that the people were unwarlike; indeed, if Syllaeus had not betrayed him, he would even have subdued the whole of Arabia Felix.

But the Aethiopians, emboldened by the fact that a part of the Roman force in Aegypt had been drawn away with Aelius Gallus when he was carrying on war against the Arabians, attacked the Thebais and the garrison of the three cohorts at Syene and by an unexpected onset took Syene and Elephantine and Philae, and enslaved the inhabitants, and also pulled down the statues of Caesar. But Petronius, setting out with less than 10,000 infantry and 800 cavalry against 30,000 men, first forced them to flee back to Pselchis, an Aethiopian city, and sent ambassadors to demand what they had taken, as also to ask the reasons why they had begun war; and when they said that they had been wronged by the Monarchs, he replied that these were not rulers of the country, but Caesar; and when they had requested three days for deliberation, but did nothing they should have done, he made an attack and forced them to come forth to battle; and he quickly turned them to flight, since they were badly marshalled and badly armed; for they had large shields, and those too made of raw oxhide, and as weapons some had only axes, others pikes, and others swords. Now some were driven together into the city, others fled into the desert, and others found refuge on a neighbouring island, having waded into the channel, for on account of the current the crocodiles were not numerous there. Among these fugitives were the generals of Queen Candace, who was a ruler of the Aethiopians in my time – a masculine sort of woman, and blind in one eye. These, one and all, he captured alive, having sailed after them in both rafts and ships, and he sent them forthwith down to Alexandria; and he also attacked Pselchis and captured it; and if the multitude of those who fell in the battle he added to the number of the captives, those who escaped must have been altogether few in number. From Pselchis he went to Premnis, a fortified city, after passing through the sanddunes, where the army of Cambyses was overwhelmed when a windstorm struck them; and having made an attack, he took the fortress at the first onset. After this he set out for Napata. This was the royal residence of Candace; and her son was there, and she herself was residing at a place near by. But though she sent ambassadors to treat for friendship and offered to give back the captives and the statues brought from Syene, Petronius attacked and captured Napata too, from which her son had fled, and razed it to the ground; and having enslaved its inhabitants, he turned back again with the booty, having decided that the regions farther on would be hard to traverse. But he fortified Premnis better, threw in a garrison and food for four hundred men for two years, and set out for Alexandria. As for the captives, he sold some of them as booty, and sent one thousand to Caesar, who had recently returned from Cantabria; and the others died of diseases. Meantime Candace marched against the garrison with many thousands of men, but Petronius set out to its assistance and arrived at the fortress first; and when he had made the place thoroughly secure by sundry devices, ambassadors came, but he bade them to go to Caesar; and when they asserted that they did not know who Caesar was or where they should have to go to find him, he gave them escorts; and they went to Samos, since Caesar was there and intended to proceed to Syria from there, after despatching Tiberius to Armenia. And when the ambassadors had obtained everything they pled for, he even remitted the tributes which he had imposed.

Pliny's account reads:[40]

Nevertheless in the time of his late Majesty Augustus the arms of Rome had penetrated even into those regions, under the leadership of Publius Petronius, himself also a member of the Order of Knighthood, when he was Governor of Egypt. Petronius captured the Arabian towns of which we will give a list, the ones we have found there: Pselcis, Primis, Bocchis, Cambyses' Market, Attenia and Standissis, where there is a cataract of the Nile the noise of which affects people dwelling near it with deafness; he also sacked the town of Napata. The farthest point he reached was 870 miles from Syene; but nevertheless it was not the arms of Rome that made the country a desert; Ethiopia was worn out by alternate periods of dominance and subjection in a series of wars with Egypt.

And that of Dio Cassius:[41]

About this time the Ethiopians, who dwell beyond Egypt, advanced as far as the city called Elephantine, with Candace as their leader, ravaging everything they encountered. At Elephantine, however, learning that Petronius, the governor of Egypt, was approaching, they hastily retreated before he arrived, hoping to make good their escape. But being overtaken on the road, they were defeated and thus drew him after them into their own country. There, too, he fought successfully with them, and took Napata, their capital, among other cities. This place was razed to the ground, and a garrison left at another point; for Petronius finding himself unable either to advance farther, on account of the sand and the heat, or advantageously to remain where he was with his entire army, withdrew, taking the greater part of it with him. There upon, the Ethiopians attacked the garrisons, but he again proceeded against them, rescued his own men, and compelled Candace to make terms with him.

These accounts give a clear enough description of the campaign and it is interesting to see that a forward garrison was left at Premnis, the modern Qasr Ibrim, when the main part of the Roman army returned to Egypt. A sidelight on a battle between Romans and Meroites is given in a papyrus at Milan[42] which, dated on calligraphic grounds to AD 60–94, describes an engagement in the desert between Romans and 'Ethiopians' in which a cavalry *ala* was involved. There is nothing to connect this battle with the campaigns of Petronius and its date is too late for that. It may therefore refer to an otherwise unknown battle, or is perhaps to be connected with the later expedition in the reign of Nero.

Plate 28

The well-known head of Augustus[43] found at Meroe is probably to be connected with these events and is likely to be from one of the Syene statues which were removed. The details of where it was found are not very clear, but it seems that it was found under the threshold of building No. 292[44, 45] which suggests that it must have been buried in a ceremonial way as an important trophy. The finding of such an object at Meroe must also arouse doubts about the suggestion of Napatan leadership during the period of the war with the Romans.

The matter is further complicated since in Temple T at Kawa there are blocks with the names of Akinidad and Amanishakhete which appear to be contemporary. Akinidad may therefore have been alive in her reign, as well as in that of Amanirenas, and Amanishakhete is also therefore a possible candidate for the Candace of Strabo. We also know of Amanishakhete from a cartouche on a brick recently found at Wad ben Naqa,[46] and we know that she was buried in pyramid N. 6 at Meroe. Another king, Amanikhabale, known from Meroe pyramid N. 2, from Basa,[47] and from Naqa,[48] also has his

Fig. 5

Fig. 6

name at Kawa. This strongly suggests that the kings of Meroe exercised power in the north, and, if there ever was an independent line of rulers at Napata, it is possible that they controlled only a small area round the town itself and that Meroe, by using the Bayuda and Wadi Muqaddam routes, was able to by-pass Napata and keep control of the region downstream.

Whatever the truth may be and whoever was the queen, Amanirenas or Amanishakhete, who so impressed the ancient world that the title of Candace became famous, Meroe had come into conflict with the Roman Empire and had been worsted, though, since the terms agreed by the Meroitic embassy to Samos were not unduly harsh, the Roman victory may not have been as overwhelming as literary sources make out.

Relations with Rome continued to be maintained and there is an inscription at Dakka, of the year 13 BC, put up by a Meroitic mission under a man called Harpocras which is important for chronology since it speaks of τήν κυρίαν βασίλισσαν, who was presumably a ruling queen of Meroe. Amanishakhete is the only one who can be meant here since the famous Queen Amanitare is nowhere mentioned in inscriptions without her husband Netekamani. Amanishakhete is therefore not likely to have died before 12 BC, and we can conveniently use this as an approximate date for the end of her reign and the beginning of the joint rule of Netekamani and Amanitare. Other evidence for contact with Rome can be seen in the later mission in AD 253 when Pasmun was sent by King Teqerideamani to the Romans; from a stela[49] at Faras, where *Mlawitr* is described as having been an ambassador to Rome; and from another stela from Karanog.[50] There may also have been envoys going the other way as well as the soldiers sent by Nero. In the tomb of Rameses V at Thebes is a graffito saying 'Κλαδῶς ὁ ἀποσταλεὶς εἰς Ἀιθιοπίαν καί ὁί μέτ' ἀύτων,' and the information given by Pliny and other writers suggests that a number of travellers from Roman Egypt, if not from Rome itself, went to Meroe.

Fig. 5. The name of Queen Amanishakhete written in Meroitic hieroglyphs

Fig. 6. Bronze cone from Kawa with the name of King Amanikhabale

The Temple of Isis at Philae was an important shrine for the people of the northern Meroitic territory (modern Nubia), and the annual pilgrimage to it at the winter solstice must have given rise to many meetings between Meroites and romanized Egyptians. Although it was well inside the Roman frontier, which after the Samos treaty was established at Hiera Sycami/ nos (modern Maharraqa), conditions were peaceful enough to allow of easy coming and going.

The reigns of Amanishakhete and her successors Neteka/ mani and Amanitare, who as husband and wife reigned jointly and are always named and shown together in the temple reliefs, mark a period of prosperity from the evidence of their building activity. Netekamani and Amanitare, frequently joined by one of their sons, are better known from the monuments than any other Meroitic rulers. They reconstructed the temple of Amun at Meroe,[51] and built two temples at Naqa – the Lion Temple, on which they are shown with the Prince Arikhankharer, and the Amun Temple where Prince Arikakhatani is associated with them. This prince is also mentioned on a temple at Bar/ kal,[52] where his parents repaired the Amun Temple left devast/ ated by the Roman army. Some of the inscriptions are in Egyptian and, like earlier rulers, they must have brought crafts/ men from Egypt for the purpose – cartouches with their names written in Egyptian and Meroitic hieroglyphs on a stone base for a sacred boat, found at Wad ben Naqa,[53] provided the key to the decipherment of Meroitic writing, as we shall see later.

Fig. 7

A third son, Sherkarer is also known from an extremely interesting scene engraved on a rock at Jebel Qeili in the southern Butana, which shows the king triumphing over enem/ ies, and is the most southerly Meroitic monument yet known.[54]

After the reign of Sherkarer there were apparently twenty/ one rulers until the end of the Meroitic kingdom, but the only event known to us during the whole period is the expedition, or perhaps two expeditions, sent in the middle of the first

Fig. 7. King Sherkarer smiting his enemies. Rock carving from Jebel Qeili (after Kush, VII)

century AD by the Emperor Nero (see p. 20). This is indicative of continued Roman interest in the area, where contact of a commercial kind already existed. Throughout the first and second centuries AD there was a steady trickle of Roman luxury goods to Meroe – some of these have been found in the royal burials and a more detailed study of them might provide further chronological checks.[55] Unfortunately, neither of the Roman accounts gives the name of the ruler of Meroe when the expedition arrived at that town, but Pliny says a queen was ruling and that there had been forty-five rulers before her.

From this time on there is a clear degeneration of Meroitic power. The royal burials are poorer, brick takes the place of stone in the construction of the pyramids, and imported objects are no longer found in these tombs. Though contact was maintained with Roman Egypt, as graffiti at Philae show, the control over the northern part of the kingdom must have become very tenuous. The only firm date is for Teqerideamani. His date is given by a demotic graffito at Philae,[56] which records that in the third year of the Emperor Trebonianus Gallus, AD 253, Teqerideamani sent an embassy with gifts to the temple of Philae. A further check is given by another Philae graffito,[57] where the king's son, Abratoi, records in AD 260 that he went to Philae to represent his father. We know therefore that Teqerideamani was reigning from before AD 253 to after AD 260.

The usually accepted date for the end of the Meroitic state has been *c.* AD 350. This date is based on an inscription of King Aezanes (*c.* AD 325–375) at Axum, which has been taken to be a description of the defeat of Meroe by an Axumite army. There are many reasons for thinking this date is too late, and recent studies[58] suggest that Meroe may well have ceased to be of importance by the time the army of Aezanes marched through the Butana. The text of the inscription is as follows:[59]

Through the might of the Lord of Heaven, who is victorious in Heaven and on earth over all! Aezanes, the son of Ella-Amida, of the tribe Halen, the king of Axum and Himyar and of Raidan and of Saba and of Salhen and of Siyamo and of Bega and of Kasu, the King of Kings, the son of Ella-Amida, who will not be defeated by the enemy. Through the might of the Lord of Heaven, who has created me, of the Lord of All by whom the king is beloved, who

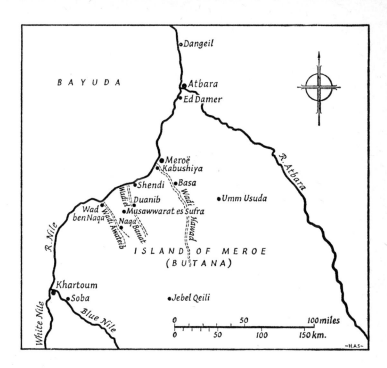

Fig. 8. The
Island of Meroe

will not be defeated by the enemy, no foe shall stand before
me and behind me no foe shall follow.

Through the might of the Lord of All I took the field
against the Noba, when the people of the Noba revolted,
when they boasted and 'He will not cross over the Takazze',
said the people of the Noba, when they did violence to the
peoples of Mangurto and Hasa and Barya. And the Blacks
waged war on the Red Peoples and a second and a third time
broke their oath, and without consideration slew their neighbours and plundered our envoys and our messengers whom
I had sent to interrogate them, robbing them of their possess-
ions and seizing their lances. When I sent again and they
did not hear me, and reviled me and made off, I took the
field against them. And I armed myself with the power of

the Lord of the land, and fought on the Takkaze at the ford of Kemalke. And thereupon they fled and stood not still, and I pursued the fugitives twenty-three days, slaying some of them and capturing others and taking booty from them, where I came; while prisoners and booty were brought back by my people who marched out; while I burnt their towns, those of masonry and those of straw, and my people seized their corn and their bronze and the dried meat and the images in their temples and destroyed the stocks of corn and cotton. And the enemy plunged into the river Seda, and there were many who perished in the water, the number I know not. And as their vessels foundered a multitude of people, men and women, were drowned. And I took prisoners two chief-tains who had come to spy, riding on camels, and their names were Yesaka and Butale, also a man of noble birth Angabenawi; and the following chieftains fell: Danokue, Dagale, Anakue, Hawarel, Karkara, and their priest, the soldiers had wounded him and taken from him a silver crown and a gold ring; it was thus five chieftains who fell, and the priest.

And I arrived at the Kasu, slaying some of them and taking others prisoner at the junction of the rivers Seda and Takkaze. And on the day after my arrival I despatched into the field the troop Mahaza and the Hara troop, and the Damawa and the Falha and Sera up the Seda against the towns of masonry and of straw; their towns of masonry are called Alwa and Daro. And they slew and took prisoners and threw them into the water, and they returned safe and sound after they had terrified their enemies and had con-quered through the power of the Lord of the Land. And I sent the troop Halen and the troop Laken and the troop Sabarat and Falba and Sera down the Seda against the towns of straw of the Noba, four, Negues, one. The towns of masonry of the Kasu which the Noba had taken were Tabito and Fertoti; and they arrived at the territory of the Red Noba, and my people returned safe and sound after they had taken some prisoners and slain others and had seized their booty through the power of the Lord of Heaven.

And I erected a throne at the junction of the rivers Seda and Takkaze, opposite the town of masonry which is on this peninsula. The Lord of Heaven has given me: male prisoners, 214, female prisoners, 415; total 629. The men slain 602; woman and children slain 156; total 758. And that is prisoners and dead, 1387. And booty about 10,500 cattle and 60, and about 51,050 sheep. And I erected a throne here in Sado through the power of the Lord of Heaven who has helped me and has given me dominion. The Lord of Heaven strengthens my dominion. And as he now has conquered my enemy, so may he conquer for me, where I go. As he now has given me victory and has overthrown my enemies, so will I rule in right and justice, doing no wrong to the peoples. And I placed the throne, which I had set up, and the earth which bears it, in the protection of the Lord of Heaven who has made me king, and if there is one who obliterates it and destroys it and tears it down, he and his line shall be uprooted and torn asunder; of them no trace shall remain in the land. And I set up this throne through the power of the Lord of Heaven.

From this it is reasonably clear that Aezanes was king of Kasu (i.e. Meroe) before the campaign began, and that the campaign was not to destroy Meroe, but to put down a revolt by the Noba, who were in possession of the Island of Meroe. Evidence for an earlier Axumite raid on Meroe, is perhaps to be found in a fragmentary inscription found there.[60] This fragment, written in Greek, is certainly of Axumite origin and *Fig. 9* since the god Ares is mentioned it must be dated before the conversion of Aezanes to Christianity in AD 350. Too little remains of the text to make much sense, but since the normal protocol given to Aezanes is not there, it may belong to one of his predecessors and therefore be prior to AD 325. Axumite pressure may well have weakened Meroe, but there is no direct evidence for capture of the town, and it might well be argued from Aezanes' inscription that it was the Noba who were the prime cause of the decline.

The late third century was a period of disengagement by the Romans, and Diocletian's calling in of the Nobatae (perhaps the same as, or related to, the Noba) in AD 296 to protect the southern frontier of Roman Egypt is symptomatic of this. That it led to an increasing isolation and impoverishment of Meroe is clearly seen in the archaeological record, most notably by the decline in the standard of building of royal pyramids. This economic decline, possible Axumite pressure, and an invasion by the Noba are quite sufficient to have ended Meroitic rule.

There is some archaeological evidence for the arrival of a new people on the scene in the third century. The late cemetery, No. 300, at Meroe shows a completely new type of burial to-gether with a new pottery of markedly African type, in sharp contrast to the fine Roman-influenced wares characteristic of earlier Meroitic ceramic art. These burials, and their associated material, are similar to those excavated at Ushara, just south of Omdurman,[61] and the much bigger ones at Tanqasi.[62] And it can be assumed that the very large number, many hundreds, of similar mounds on the west bank of the Nile are also of this people and date. It seems likely that, at some time in the second half of the third century, a people who were the Noba of the Axumite inscription moved from Kordofan in the south-west to the river valley and overran the territory of Meroe.

After the end of the third century, Meroitic power was over. Its culture continued in a somewhat altered form in that of the X-Group people of the north, known mainly from the excava-tions of royal burials at Ballana and Qostol.[63] These people occupied Lower Nubia, at least as far south as Firka, where

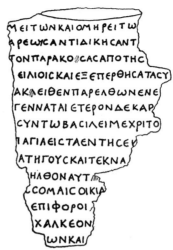

ΜΕΙΤWΝΚΑΙΟΜΗΡΕΙΤW
ΑΡΕWΚΑΝΤΙΔΙΚΗCΑΝΤ
ΤΟΝΠΑΡΑΚΟΨCΑCΑΠΟΤΗC
ΕΙΛΙΟΙCΚΑΙΕΞΕΠΕΡΘΗCΑΤΑCΥ
ΑΚΜΕΙΘΕΝΠΑΡΕΛΘWΝΕΝΕ
ΓΕΝΝΑΤΑΙΕΤΕΡΟΝΔΕΚΑΡ
CΥΝΤWΒΑCΙΛΕΙΜΕΧΡΙΤΟ
ΙΑΓΙΑΕΙCΤΑΕΝΤΗCΕΥ
ΑΤΗΓΟΥCΚΑΙΤΕΚΝΑ
ΗΛΘΟΝΑΥΤΜ
CΟΜΑΙCΟΙΚΙΑ
ΕΠΙΦΟΡΟΙ
ΧΑΛΚΕΟΝ
WΝΚΑΙ

Fig. 9. Axumite inscription in Greek from Meroe (after Soc. Bib. Arch.)

other rich mound burials have been excavated,[64] from about the beginning of the fourth century until the introduction of Christianity in the middle of the sixth century brought about cultural changes. The X-Group people are not identical with those here assumed to be the Noba,[65] though they are at least in part contemporary with them, and somewhere between Firka and Tanqasi there may have been a cultural, perhaps also a political and linguistic, frontier. We know nothing of events in the area of Meroe during this period, though on present knowledge we must assume that the Noba dwelt there until they too were converted by the missionary Longinus in AD 580.

When Longinus came into the Island of Meroe, he found the capital of the Noba(?) at Alwa, the modern Soba. Alwa has already been mentioned in the Aezanes inscription, and though some propose that this refers to the town of Meroe, it seems more likely that Soba, known throughout medieval times as Alwa, is meant. This move of the centre of political power suggests that Meroe had been so destroyed that it was no longer a suitable place for a ruler's residence.

CHRONOLOGY OF THE MEROITIC RULERS

NAME	PYRAMID	DATE
1 Kashta	Ku. 8	c. 706–751 BC
2 Piankhy	Ku. 17	751–716
3 Shabako	Ku. 15	716–701
4 Shebitku	Ku. 18	701–690
5 Taharqa	Nu. 1	690–664
6 Tanwetamani	Ku. 16	664–653
7 Atlanersa	Nu. 20	653–643
8 Senkamanisken	Nu. 3	643–623
9 Anlamani	Nu. 6	623–593
10 Aspelta	Nu. 8	593–568
11 Amtalqa	Nu. 9	568–555
12 Malenaqen	Nu. 5	555–542
13 Analmaye	Nu. 18	542–538

HINTZE

NAME	PYRAMID	DATE
14 Amani-nataki-lebte	Nu. 10	538–519 BC
15 Karkamani	Nu. 7	519–510
16 Amaniastabarqa	Nu. 2	510–487
17 Siaspiqa	Nu. 4	487–468
18 Nasakhma	Nu. 19	468–463
19 Malewiebamani	Nu. 11	463–435
20 Talakhamani	Nu. 16	435–431
21 Amani-nete-yerike	Nu. 12	431–405
22 Baskakeren	Nu. 17	405–404
23 Harsiotef	Nu. 13	404–369
24 Unknown king?	Ku. 1	369–350
25 Akhratan	Nu. 14	350–335
26 Nastasen	Nu. 15	335–310
27 Amanibakhi??	Nu. ?	310–295
28 Arakakamani	Beg. S. 6	295–275
29 Amanislo	Beg. S. 5	275–260
30 Queen Bartare	Beg. S. 10	260–250
31 Amani...tekha?	Beg. N. 4	250–235
32 Arnekhamani	Beg. N. 53	235–218
33 Arqamani	Beg. N. 7	218–200
34 Tabirqa?	Beg. N. 9	200–185
35 ...iwal??	Beg. N. 8	185–170
36 Queen Shanakdakhete	Beg. N. 11	170–160
37 Unknown king	Beg. N. 12	160–145

Note

Arikharer son of Netekamani is shown as king on tablet from Meroe (Plate 11) but has not been included in the list. He was buried in pyramid Beg. N. 5.

? and ?? means reading of name uncertain.

( ) means identification with a tomb uncertain but probable.

(( )) means identification with a tomb is only a guess.

NAME	PYRAMID	DATE	EVENTS
			Burials at Meroe from this date
			Invasion of Psammetichus II 591 BC
			Aspelta first royal name at Meroe
			Name at Meroe
			Name at Meroe

DUNHAM

NAME	PYRAMID	DATE	EVENTS
14 Amani-nataki-lebte	Nu. 10	538–520 BC	Name at Meroe
			Cambyses 525 BC
15 Karkamani	Nu. 7	520–511	
16 Amaniastabarqa	Nu. 2	511–489	
17 Siaspiqa?	Nu. 4	489–471	
18 Nasakhma	Nu. 19	471–466	
19 Malewiebamani	Nu. 11	466–439	
20 Talakhamani	Nu. 16	439–435	Died at Meroe. Given as pre-decessor of No. 21 in Kawa IX
21 Amani-nete-yerike	Nu. 12	435–417	First mention of Meroe.
22 Baskakeren	Nu. 17	417–416	
23 Harsiotef	Nu. 13	416–398	Year 35 known: Royal Palace at Napata sanded up.
24 Unknown king?	Ku. 1	398–367	
25 Akhratan	Nu. 14	367–355	
26 Nastasen	Nu. 15	335–337	Last certain burial at Nuri. Fought Khabbash c. 335 BC?
26b Amanibakhi?	Nu. ?	337–322	
27 (Arnekhamani)	Bar. 11	322–315	
28 Arakakamani	Beg. S. 6	315–297	
29 Amanislo	Beg. S. 5	297–284	
30 Queen Bartare	Beg. S. 10	284–275	
31 Aman...tekha?	Beg. N. 4	275–263	
32 (...pnayka?)	Beg. N. 53	263–248	
33 Ergamenes	Beg. N. 7	248–220	
34 Tabirqa?	Beg. N. 9	220–203	
35 Unknown king	Beg. N. 8	203–186	
36 (Nahirqa)	Beg. N. 11	186–177	
37 Queen (Shanakdakhete)	Beg. N. 12	177–155	First dateable inscription in Meroitic.

CHRONOLOGY OF THE MEROITIC RULERS (continued)

NAME		PYRAMID	DATE
38	(Naqrinsan)??	Beg. N. 13	145–120
39	((Tanyidamani))	Beg. N. 20	120–100
40	((...khale))	Beg. N. 21	100– 80
41	((..amani))??	Beg. N. 14	80– 65
42	(Amanikhabale)	Beg. N. 2	65– 41
43	Queen Amanishakhete	Beg. N. 6	41– 12
44	Netakamani	Beg. N. 22	12BC–AD12
45	Queen Amanitare	Beg. N. 1	12BC–AD12
46	(Sherkarer)	Beg. N. 10	AD12– 17
47	((Pisakar))	Beg. N. 15	17– 35
48	Amanitaraqide	Beg. N. 16	35– 45
49	Amanitenmemide	Beg. N. 17	45– 62
50	Queen Amanikhatashan	Beg. N. 18	62– 85
51	Tarekeniwal	Beg. N. 19	85–103
52	((Amanikhalika))	Beg. N. 32	103–108
53	(Aritenyesbekhe)	Beg. N. 34	108–132
54	((Aqrakamani))	Beg. N. 40	132–137
55	((Adeqetali))	Beg. N. 41	137–146
56	Takideamani	Beg. N. 29	146–165
57	((..reqerem))?	Beg. N. 30	165–184
58	...	Beg. N. 37	184–194
59	((Teritedakhatey))	Beg. N. 38	194–209
60	Aryesbekhe	Beg. N. 36	209–228
61	Teritnide	Beg. N. 51	228–246
62	Aretnide	Beg. N. 35	246
63	Teqerideamani	Beg. N. 28	246–266
64	((Tamelerdeamani))?	Beg. N. 27	266–283
65	((Yesbekheamani))?	Beg. N. 24	283–300
66	((Lakhideamani))??	Beg. N. 26	300–308
67	((Maleqerebar))?	Beg. N. 25	308–320

NAME	PYRAMID	DATE	EVENTS
38 (Naqrinsan)??	Beg. N. 13	155–133	
39 ((Tanyidamani))	Beg. N. 20	133–116	
40 ((Teriteqas))	Beg. N. 21	116– 99	
41 ((Amanirenas))	Bar. 4	99– 84	
42 ((Akinidad))	Bar. 2	84– 69	
43 Unknown king	Beg. N. 14	69– 56	
44 Naldamak	Bar. 6	56– 43	
45 (Amanikhabale)	Beg. N. 2	43– 26	
46 Queen Amanishakhete	Beg. N. 6	26– 20	Roman invasion 23 BC
47 Unknown king	Bar. 9	20– 10	
48 Unknown queen	Bar. 10	10– 0	
49 Natakamani	Beg. N. 22	AD 0– 25	
50 Queen Amanitare	Beg. N. 1	25– 41	
51 (Sherkarer)	Beg. N. 10	41– 45	
52 ((Teritedakhatey))	Beg. N. 15	45– 62	
53 Aryesbekhe	Beg. N. 16	62– 78	
54 Amanitenmemide	Beg. N. 17	78– 93	
55 Queen Amanikhatashan	Beg. N. 18	83–115	
56 Unknown king	Beg. N. 40	115–119	
57 ((..r.keniwal))	Beg. N. 41	119–128	
58 (Aritenyesbekhe)	Beg. N. 34	128–150	
59 Takideamani	Beg. N. 29	150–167	
60 Unknown king	Beg. N. 30	167–184	
61 Tarekenidal	Beg. N. 19	184–201	
62 Unknown queen	Beg. N. 32	201–205	
63 ...	Beg. N. 37	205–214	
64 ((Pisapade))	Beg. N. 38	214–228	
65 Amanitaraqide	Beg. N. 36	228–246	
66 Teqerideamani	Beg. N. 28	246–266	
67 ...	Beg. N. 35	266	
68 Unknown king	Beg. N. 51	266–283	
69 Unknown king	Beg. N. 24	283–300	
70 Unknown king	Beg. N. 27	300–317	
71 Unknown queen	Beg. N. 26	317–326	
72 Unknown king	Beg. N. 25	326–339	

CHAPTER III
Towns, Temples, and Cemeteries

MEROITIC CIVILIZATION, like that of Pharaonic Egypt, was based on the river Nile. Although in the Island of Meroe itself it was possible to build away from the river, it was still the Nile which formed the main unifying element, and along whose banks the main centres of Meroitic power and culture flourished. The greatest limits of Meroitic occupation, so far as present knowledge goes, were from near Dakka[1] in Egyptian Nubia to as far south as Sennar, far up the Blue Nile. This is a distance of some 700 miles as the crow flies; along the river, the route by which communication would normally have been maintained, it is very much longer.

For a great deal of this distance, the only cultivable land is a narrow strip beside the river. This strip, often only a hundred yards or so wide, is characteristic of Nubia, from the northern Meroitic boundary in modern Egypt to as far south as the junc, tion of the Atbara with the Nile. On either side stretches desert, running on the east to the hills which border the Red Sea and on the west through the sands of the Libyan desert and across the Sahara to the Atlantic. In the desert only nomads can survive, and, although they too had their influence on the history of the Nile Valley, and no doubt Meroe had influence on them, Meroe was essentially a civilization of the settled people of the river banks.

South of Dakka the river runs through inhospitable country, but its original appearance has been much changed since the building of the first Aswan dam and its subsequent heighten, ing. In this area there are no sites of Napatan or early Meroitic times. Of the cemeteries and settlements found by the survey expeditions, which have worked over the area in an attempt to record the antiquities before they were submerged by the various floodings,[2] little is earlier than the first century AD,[3] and it was probably only after the introduction of the *saqia*, the ox-driven water-wheel, in the second or third centuries BC, that cultivation was possible here.

The Dodecaschoenus, the province immediately up-stream of Philae, seems to have remained in Ptolemaic or Roman hands almost throughout, and no traces of Meroitic settlement have been found north of the cemetery at Garba, just south of Maharraqa.[4] Temporary military occupation there may have been, and the troubles which Ptolemy IV Philopator and Ptolemy V Epiphanes had in Upper Egypt may well have allowed a short Meroitic incursion in the time of Arqamani, since he left his name at Philae as well as building at Dakka. By the nineteenth year of Ptolemy V Epiphanes, Egyptian rule had again been established over the Dodecaschoenus and the only other Meroitic incursion seems to have been that of 23 BC. After that the Roman frontier, like the Ptolemaic one before it, was firmly established at Hiera Sycaminos, the modern Maharraqa.[5]

Arqamani's chapel at Dakka, the ancient Pselchis, is thus the most northerly Meroitic monument. The chapel forms a part of a temple, the other portions of which were added at later times. Several Ptolemies built here and the forecourt is a Roman addition.[6] Since Ptolemy IV, who was a contemporary of Arqamani, also built here there must have been some co-operation between Meroe and Ptolemaic Egypt.

South of Wadi es-Sebua traces of Meroitic occupation become much more common, and Emery and Kirwan[7] suggest that the large settlement at this point, connected with their cemetery No. 150, was the real frontier town. From here southwards, by the beginning of the second century AD a number of small settlements existed,[8] but at this northern limit of Meroitic territory, there are none of the towns and temples found further south. Most of the cemeteries must have been associated with villages like that at Shablul.[9]

Karanog, near the modern town of Aniba and opposite the great fort of Qasr Ibrim, seems to have been a more important centre, but most of the surviving buildings in the town are post-Meroitic as are those at Qasr Ibrim. The cemetery discovered there seems also to be late, nothing in it being earlier than the first century AD.[10] The same can be said of the recently excavated cemetery at Toshka where the one inscription found is of the third century AD.[11] Further south, are the remains of a small town north of Abu Simbel belonging to the very end of the Meroitic period.[12]

Fig. 10

Just over the Sudan border, where there is rather more cultivable land, is the important site of Faras.[13] This site, in Meroitic *Pakhoras*,[14] formerly an island but now by a change in the course of the Nile standing on its west bank, was the capital of the Meroitic province of *Akin,* covering Lower Nubia, and ruled by a viceroy with the title of *Pesate*.[15]

The Meroitic remains consist of a large cemetery in which over 2,000 graves were excavated, and it is from this cemetery and the wealth of material found that Griffith evolved a typo-

Fig. 11

logy and chronology of the graves which, until recently, has been our only guide for dating the pottery. The graves were of three

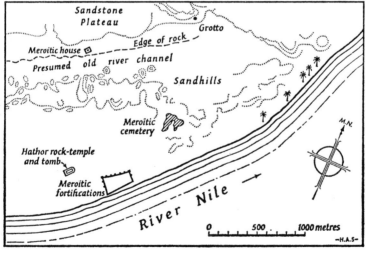

Fig. 10. Map of Faras

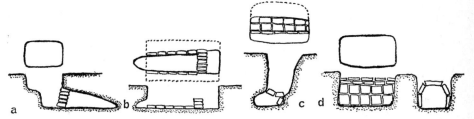

Fig. 11.   *Grave types at Faras: (a) cave grave; (b) foot niche grave; (c) lateral niche grave; (d) rectangular grave*

main types, the earliest of which, called by Griffith 'cave graves', date from late Ptolemaic times. They consisted of a stepped shaft with a cave-like burial chamber to one side, the entrance being usually blocked with stone or broken brick. In the earlier of the two sub-types, 'anklet graves', the bodies were buried with their feet towards the entrance, in a position not otherwise known later than the Napatan period. The term 'anklet grave' was used because the bodies frequently had bronze pennanular anklets, similar to the heavy silver ones worn today by some Sudanese women. Apart from the anklets little was found in the graves. The second and later sub-type of cave grave had its opening to the west and the body was placed with its head to the entrance. Anklets were not found but pottery and other antiquities were present in some quantity.

The second main type, the 'niche grave', again took two forms, one having the niche at the foot, the so-called 'foot niche' graves; the second with the niche at the side, known as 'lateral niche' graves, had the extra feature of a flat or vaulted brick roof. All these graves seem to date from the first and second centuries AD.

The last type, 'rectangular graves', were rectangular pits with brick-lined sides, some of which contained more than one body, and were all rich in antiquities, pottery being extremely plenti- ful. Examples of this type were very common at Faras and they represent the latest true Meroitic graves.

Fig. 11

In addition to these main types, a few graves at Faras were found with square brick-built superstructures and a shrine against the east wall. Similar graves had been found at Shablul and Aniba, where the excavators considered them to be masta-bas.[16] It seems more likely that they are the remains of pyramids.

The main town site has not been identified, but some official buildings were found and excavated. One of these, the 'Western Palace', lay on the western edge of the site and presumably stood on what was the western bank of a now dried-up branch of the river. The building, of sun-dried brick, consisted of a pillared courtyard, surrounded by a series of small rooms and enclosing a central building. From the objects found in it, it can be dated to about the first century AD or a little earlier.

The great wall round the main mound, under which was recently found a cathedral of the eighth century AD,[17] was re-used and modified in Christian times. The wall itself was built of small sandstone blocks up to a height of about four metres, and above that of sun-dried brick for another eight metres. Evid-

Fig. 12

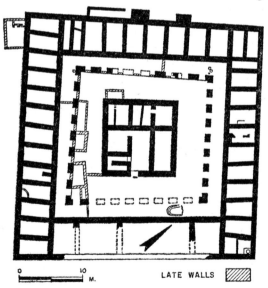

Fig. 12. Plan of the Western Palace, Faras (after Liver-pool Annals, XIII)

LATE WALLS

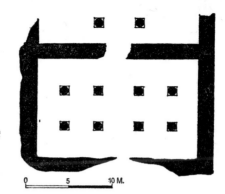

Fig. 13. Plan of the temple at
Amara East (after Budge)

0   5   10 M.

ence of Meroitic buildings of some importance is to be found
in the many cut stone blocks which were re-used in Christian
times in the cathedral walls and doorways.

In the area immediately south of Faras, Meroitic remains are
rare, but cemeteries have been found at Aksha and Argin.[18]
Just before the rugged and inhospitable area of the Second
Cataract, on the east bank of the river, is the rich cemetery of
Gemai.[19] At this point the rocks reduce the width of the Nile
to a mere hundred yards in some places and form a natural
boundary, where in earlier times the Pharaohs of the Egyptian
Middle Kingdom established their frontier and built a series of
massive forts to keep out the southern barbarians. In this region
too there is little evidence of Meroitic occupation, although one
of the very few Meroitic houses to be discovered there was excavated at Gaminarti in the last few years,[20] and a block with a
cartouche of a Meroitic king, probably Amanislo,[21] and a few
Meroitic objects have been found in the fort at Semna.

From here southwards, the country remains equally inhospitable – it is appropriately known in Arabic as the *Batn el-hagar,*
'The belly of the rocks' – until, beyond Firka, the rocks lie
further from the river, allowing more extensive cultivation.

A few miles upstream stood the temple of Amara of which
no trace now remains, although it was seen and described by
several travellers during the last century.[22] Budge also described

Fig. 13

it,[23] though it is clear that it cannot have been standing when he visited the area.[24] A plan of the temple is given by Lepsius[25] and shows it to have consisted of a chamber with eight columns and an outer court with at least two more columns. It is of importance as having the names of Netekamani, Amanitare, and Prince Sherkarer in the inscriptions on the columns[26] and is the most northerly record of this king as well as the most northerly inscription in Meroitic hieroglyphs. It seems to have been dedicated to the god Amun.[27]

Plate 23

Fig. 14

South again towards Dongola there are wider lands and in- creased signs of ancient occupation. On the large island of Argo are two colossal statues, probably of King Netekamani,[28] which must have stood on either side of the main entrance to a temple, the much ruined remains of which can just be identi- fied. The next important site, opposite the modern town of Dongola, is Kawa, where stood temples and a large town with

Fig. 14. Plan of the temples at Kawa (after Macadam)

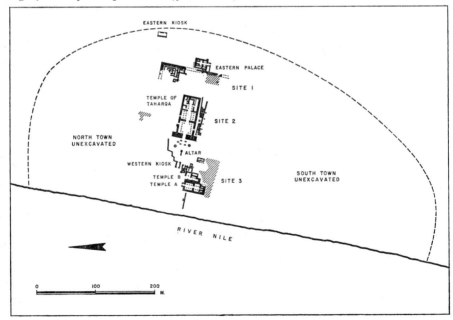

Fig. 15.   Reliefs on the pylon of temple B, Kawa, showing Amun-Re and other gods (after Macadam)

a long history going back to New Kingdom times.[29] The temples are in the main pre-Meroitic, most of the building having been carried out by Taharqa; but there is some purely Meroitic building, as for example the columns in the outer court of Temple B, erected by Harsiotef. The sanctuary of this temple and the pylons at the entrance are later. The figures in the reliefs lack the usual Meroitic obesity and steatopygy and have a strong Ptolemaic flavour which would date them to the third century BC. Temple A, although founded in the XVIII Dynasty and reconstructed by Taharqa, was certainly in use in Meroitic times, and the name of King Arnekhamani subse-quently known from Musawwarat es-Sofra, was first found in the sanctuary here on a bronze head of Isis. The temple seems to have been re-floored in the first century BC, perhaps in the reign of Amanishakhete, and a stela of Aryamani was found re-used in the floor.

Temple T, the great temple of Taharqa, was likewise in use in Meroitic times and Aspelta built a shrine within the hypo-style hall.[30] There are a number of inscriptions of Meroitic

Fig. 15

Plate 36

kings, including the great inscription of Amani-nete-yerike, as well as graffiti in Meroitic cursive.

Some building was carried out here in the time of Amanis-hakhete who, together with Akinidad, left her name on a sandstone block.

The so-called 'Eastern Palace', a rectangular brick building, was also clearly Meroitic; perhaps of the first century BC. The stone entrance was flanked by small recumbent lions of red sandstone, and from this and the plan it could well have been a temple, possibly dedicated to the Lion-god Apedemek.

Owing to the ruinous nature of the buildings, excavations in the residential part of the town revealed little but they established that there was occupation up to at least the end of the third century AD, when the town and temples seem to have been severely damaged by fire.

Fig. 16

Up-stream of Kawa there are no sites of importance until Napata is reached, though a few small sites and stray objects have been recorded. The map shows the location of the sites in this homeland of Napatan and early Meroitic times. Though the town site of Napata remains undiscovered, the royal cemeteries at Kurru, Nuri and Jebel Barkal, the temples of Jebel Barkal, and the temple at Sanam have all been explored.

Since the Kurru cemetery[31] is entirely Napatan, Tanwetamani having been the last ruler to be buried there, it need not be described here. At Nuri are the earliest Meroitic royal burials, although even here, in accordance with the arbitrary chronological line we have drawn, the first four royal burials must be regarded as Napatan. Taharqa was the first to be buried there, although there was a return to Kurru for the burial of his successor. The cemetery[32] is about six miles up-stream of the modern town of Karima and stands on the opposite (i.e. left, or east) bank.[33] On two small ridges about a mile from the river stand eighty-two separate tombs, the great majority, perhaps all, of which were pyramids. This was a reversion to a

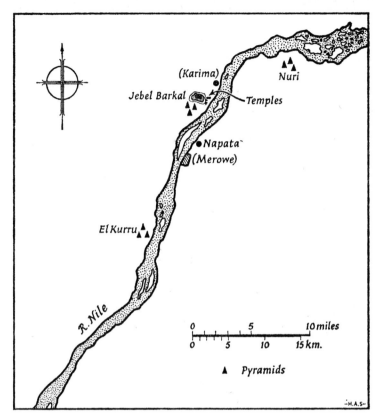

Fig. 16.   The Napata area

method of royal burial common in the Egyptian Old Kingdom and occurring later but which had not been used for royal burials since the beginning of the XVIII Dynasty.[34] These new Kushite pyramids appear first at Kurru, where the earliest is that of Piankhy. The small size and sharply pointed shape of most of them suggests that the inspiration came from the private pyramids used extensively in Egypt from the XVIII Dynasty, and known particularly from Deir el-Medina.[35] These pyra-mids continued to be built until at least the XX Dynasty and may have occurred in Kush, for the tomb of Amenemhat at

Fig. 17

Sheikh Oweis el-Quruny near Serra of the XIX Dynasty was probably surmounted by such a pyramid.[36] A typical Meroitic pyramid with its chapel and burial chamber is shown below.

It can be observed that the first pyramid, that of Taharqa, stands in what must have been the most dominant and favourable position on the ridge, and that each subsequent one was built on the best remaining site. In addition to this geographical arrangement, the pyramids fall into several clearly differentiated typological groups which are analysed in detail by Dunham[37] with charts to show the time range of different types. This analysis is not only concerned with the construction of the pyramids themselves, but also of the chapels, the access to burial, entrance doorways, burial chambers, and methods of burial.

This cemetery was in use from the time of Taharqa until that of Nastasen, after which royal burials were at Meroe, except perhaps for a few at Barkal. All the pyramids are now in a ruinous state since not only were they built of a soft sandstone which has weathered very badly but were also plundered and damaged in ancient times.

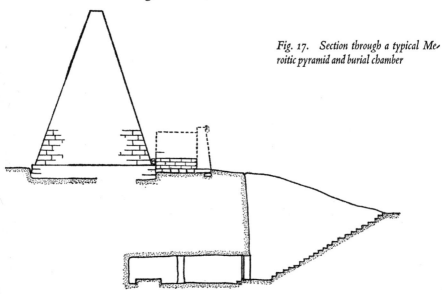

Fig. 17. Section through a typical Meroitic pyramid and burial chamber

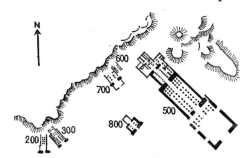

Fig. 18. The Jebel Bar-kal area (after Budge)

The site of the town of Napata has not been certainly identi-fied although it is probably on the left bank and immediately north of the modern town of Merowe. There are considerable traces of occupation, a temple, and a large cemetery, all of which were excavated by Griffith.[38] The greater part of the remains are of Napatan date and the temple was built by Taharqa, but there are traces of later work; Aspelta erected a shrine here and there is one block with the name of Malewiebamani.

Across the river is the massive hill known as Jebel Barkal, rising some 300 feet above the plain. It is a notable landmark and must have been regarded as sacred from early times. At its foot on the river side are a series of important temples and a small group of pyramids. The site consists of several temples most easily identified by the numbers given to them by Reis-ner.[39] Although No. 500, the great temple of Amun, was begun in the New Kingdom, the main period of building was in Napatan times, much of it by Piankhy and Taharqa. There was a considerable amount of restoration and some new build-ing by Meroitic rulers during the partial restoration of the sixth century BC. Continuous use of the temple over a long period is shown by the occurrence in it of stelae of Aspelta, Harsiotef, Tanyidamani, and Queen Sakhmak, wife of Nastasen. The outer court (No. 501) appears to date from Meroitic times (per-haps 300–100 BC). The name of Netekamani is given on the

Fig. 18

73

entrance of the inner vestibule (No. 506) and the excavator considered that the very latest restoration took place in his time.

Temple No. 600 is a small chapel of Meroitic date using blocks from a temple of Tuthmosis IV which must have stood on the same site. It consists of an inner room with a low plat⁄form approached by a stair, an outer room with four columns, and a portico with eight.

South of No. 600 and the Napatan temple No. 700 lie two other small temples partly of Meroitic date, numbered 800 and 900. They were probably built by Piankhy but were modified and added to in the first century BC. In room No. 904, a cache of twenty fragments of granite statues of Taharqa, Tanweta⁄mani, Senkamanisken, Anlamani and Aspelta were found. Since a number of fragments from the great temple (No. 500) were found to fit these it has been assumed that the statues all originally stood there. It would seem that these statues had been deliberately broken in temple No. 500 and, since the latest statue was of Aspelta, it is tempting to see in this destruction a reflection of the attack on Napata by Psammetichus II in 591 BC.[40]

In addition to these temples, there is also the group of neigh⁄bouring pyramids, which has posed a number of problems of chronology (see p. 39). Most of these pyramids can be ap⁄proximately fitted into the chronological scheme, but in only one case, Queen Naldamak of pyramid 6, can a definite name be given to the owner of the tomb.

Up⁄stream from Napata there is a long stretch of country, through the rocky and wild Fourth Cataract and beyond to Dangeil, five miles north of Berber, in which no Meroitic sites are at present known. Dangeil,[41] which has produced one Me⁄roitic inscription,[42] seems to have been a town of some size, and as well as the remains of the town, there is a large rectangular walled enclosure 318 paces long by 144 paces wide, the walls being made of sun⁄dried bricks faced with burnt brick. It is from these that the site takes its name, the word being a local one meaning 'red brick'.[43] There are a number of other sites, all small, none of which have yet been fully examined.[44]

South of the point where the Atbara joins the Nile the country changes, and we reach the wide plains of the Butana, enclosed by the rivers Nile, Atbara, and Blue Nile, the classic Island of Meroe. Here annual rainfall makes possible a different life. In the wadis of the Butana cultivation is possible away from the river, and sheep and cattle can graze on the grass which grows abundantly. Across the western half of this plain can be found many traces of Meroitic settlement[45] and it was here that the characteristic Meroitic civilization developed. But no Meroitic sites are known from the eastern part of the Butana, confirming the impression that this civilization was essentially a riverain one.

Of all the sites of the area the town of Meroe, beside the modern village of Begarawiya, is far the most important. Capital of the country and residence of the kings from perhaps the sixth century BC to the end of the fourth century AD, the town covers a large area on the east bank of the river. East of it lie temples and cemeteries on a plain overlooked by the low hills on which stand the pyramids, the burial places of the rulers and their families.

Our knowledge of the site is mainly derived from the excavations carried out there from 1909 to 1914 by Garstang. Unfortunately only the work of the first season was published in any detail, and for the subsequent seasons we have only the brief accounts given in the *Interim Reports*.[46] The royal cemeteries, which lie some two miles to the east of the town, were excavated by Reisner and have now been completely published.[47]

For many years the exact location of the town was not known, though such early travellers as Ferlini and Bruce guessed correctly that the ruins they saw were those of the city which had

Fig. 19

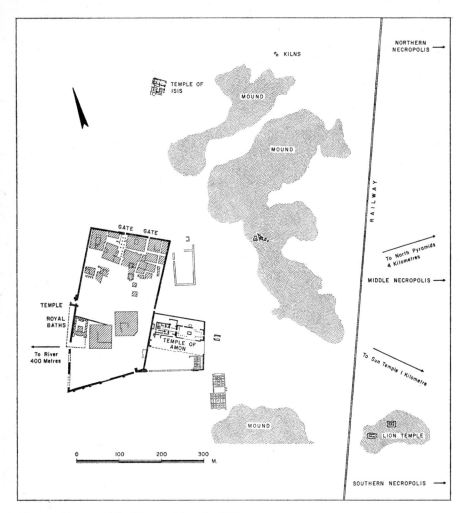

Fig. 19. Meroe town (after Liverpool Annals, VII)

been so well known in ancient times. Even Budge and Ward in 1905 were unable to say where the ruins of Meroe lay,[48] and it was not until Garstang excavated there that any certain identification could be made.[49]

The excavations were carried out in the wholesale way traditional in those days in the Nile Valley, and it is very difficult to extract from the annual reports of the excavation a proper description of those parts of the site which were excavated. Nevertheless by combining the published results with personal observation some account of this, the major site of Meroitic civilization, can be given.

The greater part of the town area, consisting of many mounds covered with red brick fragments, is still unexcavated, but in the part examined the main elements found were the temple of Amun, an enclosure containing 'palaces', a royal bath, and many other buildings called 'The Royal City' by the excavator. The Lion Temple, the Temple of Isis, and, lying east of the town, the Sun Temple, and the nonroyal cemeteries, were also cleared. The unexcavated part contains the mounds of slag from the iron working for which Meroe was famous. Six large mounds of slag and other debris of iron smelting are to be seen on the west and south edges of the town.

THE TEMPLE OF AMUN

This was the largest single building excavated. It is 450 feet long and was approached through a small kiosk or shrine, the walk from one to the other being flanked by four stone rams. The only evidence for the date of the kiosk is a reused block, with the name of Amanitare, built into the wall. The temple was constructed largely of brick, the facing bricks alone being fired, with columns, pylons, and doorways faced with dressed blocks of sandstone. It consists of an outer hall (A) of peristyle type showing signs of at least two periods of building. In the middle of the hall was a small stone shrine (B) with the names of Netekamani and Amanitare on the walls, and to the west of it a stone dais, or pulpit, with steps and engraved scenes of bound and kneeling prisoners. Beyong this court was a series

Plate 4

Fig. 20

77

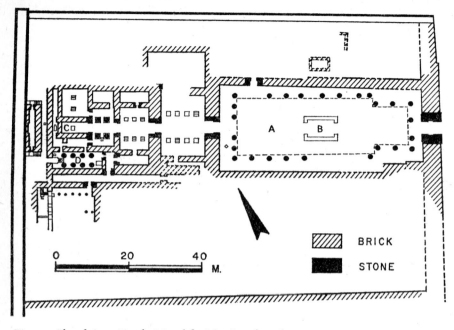

Fig. 20. Plan of Amun Temple, Meroe (after Liv. Annals, *IV)*

Plate 3 of smaller ones leading to the sanctuary (C) in which was an altar decorated with religious scenes. The so-called Hall of Columns (D) is an unusual feature and its purpose is not clear. The pillars were painted with blue and other colours on white stucco, and at the west end is a raised dais approached by a short flight of steps.

THE ROYAL CITY

Excavation was confined almost entirely to the area enclosed by a great wall on the western side of the site and immediately west of the temple of Amun. It was the presence of this wall which gave the name *es Sur* (Arabic 'wall') to the site in the early nineteenth century. Within this walled enclosure were found the remains of many buildings of different periods, some of them of considerable complexity.

In addition to buildings of a domestic nature, there was a remarkable structure usually referred to as the 'Roman Bath'. It consists of a large brick-lined tank with an elaborate system of water channels leading into it from a well near by. A ledge running round the upper part of the tank was decorated with plaster figures and medallions, as well as water spouts in the form of lion heads. All these features were painted and traces remain of frescoes on the stump of an upper wall. Both the general design and the ornate decoration strongly suggest that this was a place of recreation, and it must surely have been a swimming bath, a provincial variant of the well-known feature of Mediterranean life of the period.

One of the buildings within the royal enclosure is of special interest since the famous head of Augustus was found in front of it in a pocket of clean sand. This building is the small temple No. 292. The description available is not very full but tells us something:

> ... its interior walls are covered with stucco and decorated in barbaric fashion with gorgeous colours. The scenes represent the King and Queen of Ethiopia, their officials, and maybe, their allies, as well as a number of captives of foreign race. In the centre of this building rose up a secondary structure which had doubtless formed the pedestal of a statue or group. The columns of the original building had been cut down, with their capitals lowered and re-used, probably to support the canopy over the statue. Unfortunately, the destruction of time had proceeded too far for anything of the statue to be traceable in situ, though the plinth of the pedestal is evident.

Recent examination reveals no trace at all of these paintings, which would seem to have disappeared during the last fifty years as a result of exposure to the weather. Garstang's description does not make it clear that there are two superimposed buildings here, and the lowered capitals to which he refers are in fact the bases for columns of a later building, standing on the truncated columns of an earlier temple. The 'secondary struct' ure' contains many re'used blocks of a style suggesting that they come from this earlier building, and from the evidence of plaster at the level of the floor of the upper building it is certain that this structure is of the later period. From the finding of Augustus' head, it is tempting to see in the later building a victory temple put up to celebrate the raid on Syene (see p. 48), and to deduce that the pedestal was originally for the statue of Augustus known to have been captured there.

In the last *Interim Report,* the excavator divided the history of the town into three periods – Early, *c.* 650–400(?) BC; Middle, 300–1 BC; and late, AD 1–350 – and made an attempt to allocate buildings to these periods. Garstang's attempts at dating were hampered by the absence of any firm knowledge of Meroitic history in his time, and also, until the last season, by the belief that Meroitic occupation continued until about AD 700. It would be of great interest to know why AD 700 was chosen but the reasons are nowhere given. It may be that such a late date was assumed because of Christian settlement which Gar' stang said that he found on the Temple of Isis mound, but nowhere else in the report is there any suggestion of post' Meroitic occupation. Plate III, 1 and 2 in the *Fourth Interim Report* show a capital of markedly Christian appearance and a vaulted room with the characteristic Nubian vault, well known from Christian times further north. This type of roofing may have been in use in Meroitic times but has nowhere been re' ported, and it may be that unwittingly these two illustrations provide evidence of post'Meroitic occupation and that the date of *c.* AD 700 may be an approximation to the date of the final abandonment of the site. On a recent visit a number of sherds of Christian pottery were collected and provide the evidence, previously lacking, for Christian occupation here.

Without re-excavation it is difficult to establish a chronology but, since we know from the excavations of the pyramids (see below) that there had been burials at Meroe from at least the seventh century BC onwards, it is reasonable to assume that the town was occupied from that date. The finding of foundation deposits of Kings Amtalqa and Malenaqen in palace No. 294 certainly suggests that this building, at least, dates in part from the sixth century. Cartouches of Amani-nataki-lebte were found near to the Amun Temple, but the only other royal names found in the town are Akinidad, whose name also appears on the Hamdab stela (see below, p. 84), Teriteqas, Netekamani, and Amanitare. Since the greater part of the finds, so far as we know them, suggest Hellenistic or Roman influence, it would seem that the main occupation of the site falls into the last two centuries BC and the first AD.

THE SUN TEMPLE

The existence of a temple at Meroe, dedicated to the worship of the sun, has been assumed from Herodotus's account of the 'Table of the Sun' and it is, perhaps, to be identified with the temple found by Garstang about a mile east of the main town. The evidence for the identification is extremely slight and it is mainly based on the finding of a block with a large solar disc on it amongst the ruins of the west wall of the sanctuary. But the use of the term 'Sun Temple' has now gained such wide acceptance that it is convenient to use it with the warning that the equation with the 'Table of the Sun' is only hypothesis.

Plates 5, 6

Fig. 21

The temple was surrounded by a *temenos* wall of red brick with stone-faced doorways as in the Amun Temple. Inside this enclosure a ramp led to a platform with a colonnade enclosing the sanctuary. The outside wall of this platform was decorated with a series of reliefs, now much disintegrated. Only a summary account was given[50] and very few illustrations were

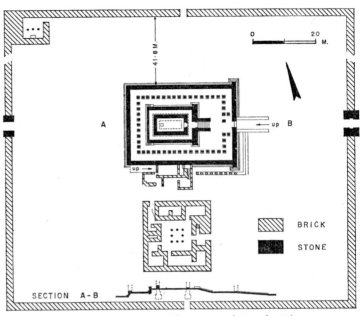

Fig. 21. Plan of Sun Temple, Meroe (after Liverpool Annals, *III)*

published, but from these it is possible to see that on the eastern façade there was a series of figures of prisoners with their bodies represented by cartouches. The cartouches of those to the north of the entrance were left blank, but those to the south have inscriptions which, by analogy with similar scenes on Egyptian temples, must be the names of conquered peoples or countries. Round the other walls are much damaged scenes of victory processions. That on the south shows Meroitic soldiers with prisoners, whilst the northern one seems to represent a seated king facing a long line of women, dancing figures, cattle, and a chariot drawn by four horses. The west wall of the corridor has reliefs showing bound prisoners beneath the royal foot. One of these prisoners is shown wearing a curious hat or helmet and several authors have tried to see in this a representation of a Greek helmet.[51]

Fig. 22

Fig. 22. Detail of relief from the Sun Temple, Meroe, showing a bound prisoner

The sanctuary was approached by a flight of stone steps, and its floors and walls were covered with blue glazed tiles. There are a number of inscriptions on the walls of the approach which seem to be written in Egyptian, though of a very debased sort.[52] That there had also been reliefs on the walls of the corridor surrounding the sanctuary is shown by a surviving portion depicting a royal figure and three cartouches which give the name of Akinidad; and comparison with reliefs at Naqa suggests that here was a scene of a king of unknown name, followed by the Prince Akinidad. This fragment of relief is different in style from the decorations on the platform and may well be a later addition or part of a rebuilding.

Fragments of a granite stela of Aspelta were found in the western part of the outer courtyard, so it may be that the temple was originally built in his time (*c.* 593–568 BC) and then restored at the end of the first century BC.

THE LION TEMPLE

This temple was built on top of an iron slag heap immediately east of where the railway now runs. It consists of two small rooms within an enclosing stone wall which is decorated with reliefs, now almost obliterated. A short flight of steps led up to the first room and was originally flanked by two stone lions, one of which was found *in situ*. It is from the presence of these lions and a stela inscribed in Meroitic found in the temple, bearing the name of the Lion-god Apedemek, that the attribution of the temple has been given. The name of King Teqeri-deamani is given on a stone statue base and is the only evidence for date. A short distance to the west and on the same mound is another small temple of which the excavator left no details.

THE TEMPLE OF ISIS

The mound which covered this building also lies outside the town proper and a little to the north of the modern village of El-Deragab. Excavation showed that there were two super-imposed buildings here, of which the later one is said to have been re-used in Christian times, that is after the sixth century AD. Both buildings appear to have been temples, though the lower one was only partly excavated. The upper building con-tained two columned halls leading to a shrine, where the altar stood on a floor of faience tiles. A stela of King Teriteqas, otherwise known only from an inscription of Dakka where he is associated with Queen Amanirenas and Prince Akinidad, was found in the upper building and may be evidence of a late first century BC date. The lower building contained two large columnar statues of a king or a god, which presumably stood on either side of the entrance to the temple. Two small figures of Isis found here are the basis for the identification of the build-ing as a temple of that goddess.

Plate 24

THE SHRINE OF APIS

This building lies about one and a half miles south of the royal enclosure well away from the main site and near the modern village of Hamdab. The dedication of the shrine is ascribed by Sayce to Apis, though the reasons are not given. Its importance lies in the discovery there of two large stelae in-scribed in Meroitic cursive. One of them, now in the British Museum, bearing the names of Amanirenas and Akinidad, is thought perhaps to give a version of the war with the Romans in 23 BC. The other stela was moved to the main site where it still is.[53]

The non-royal cemeteries lie to the east of the town across the railway, and fall into three groups: South (graves 1–99), Middle (300–399), and North (500–599).

The earliest, the northern group, contained pottery of the fine painted style known to belong to the first century BC and the first two centuries AD. The excavator incorrectly[54] assumed the southern and middle cemeteries to be the earliest on account of the coarse pottery found in them, and thought that the northern cemetery was later. The southern and middle cemeteries in fact date from a period well after the northern one, since material in them, as well as the existence of Meroitic offering tables re-used to block the entrances, shows that they belong at earliest to the very end of the Meroitic period, and they may perhaps have still been in use a century or more after the end of the Meroitic state.

These graves were all of much the same type, their burial chambers being covered with a mound of sand or gravel. The earlier graves of the northern cemetery appear to be similar to the 'cave graves' of Griffith's classification. The later graves had larger burial chambers, and the bodies had in many instances been placed on wooden beds. Ample grave goods were found, amongst which the pottery was of a type also known from the excavation of Ushara, a few miles south of Omdurman.[55] A glass bottle of Egyptian manufacture in grave 300 suggests that a date after *c.* AD 300 is likely.[56]

Many private burials are also found in the so-called royal cemeteries of Meroe further to the east, the majority of them on a ridge of sandstone hills bordering the plain.[57] There are three separate groups of tombs known as the southern, northern, and western cemeteries.[58] The southern one surmounts a spur divided by a small valley from the main ridge on which stands the northern cemetery. It consists of over two hundred graves the earliest of which dates from about the time of Piankhy (*c.* 750 BC). Most of these graves are simple pit burials of private persons, but there are also a number of mastabas and pyramids of those who were presumably members of the royal family. They certainly include the pyramids of such rulers as Arakakamani, who was the first king to be buried at Meroe, Amanislo, and perhaps Queen Bartare.

The North Cemetery was the main burial place of the rulers of Meroe and their immediate relatives and was in use from the reign of the king buried in N. 4,[59] whose name is not clearly written and appears to read Amani... tekha(?), in about the middle of the third century BC until the end of Meroitic times. The pyramids of this group are the best preserved and some of them stand virtually intact. They are not identical in style but conform to a general pattern, the variations of which have helped in determining the chronological arrangement.

The normal method of building these pyramids was to face a rubble core with dressed sandstone blocks; and then against the east face of the pyramid a chapel was built with pylons at the entrance. The walls of the chapels were covered with reliefs (see Chapter IV), and in many cases with inscriptions, and it is from these that the majority of the names of those buried have been obtained. The burial chamber was dug into the rock below the pyramid and was approached by a stairway, the entrance to which lay to the east of the chapel. This entrance was blocked and there was no indication of its presence on the surface of the ground. The stairway led to rock-cut chambers which contained the burial and the grave goods, usually three chambers in a king's tomb and two in a queen's. The later pyramids are simple and rougher and are frequently built of brick.

The West Cemetery lies on the plain a short distance to the south-west of the other two, and consists of a number of pyra-mids more ruined than those of either of the other cemeteries. In date it covers the whole period from the time of the earliest burials in the South Cemetery to the latest in the northern one. No king's tomb nor that of a reigning queen was found here amongst about five hundred graves; it is probable that members of the royal family of only secondary importance were buried here together with commoners.

A short way up-stream from Meroe is the site of Wad ben Naqa, described by Lepsius,[60] but much damaged since his time. It consists of the ruins of at least two temples, one of which was of the time of Netekamani and provided the inscription in Egyptian and Meroitic hieroglyphs which gave the first clue to the reading of Meroitic (see p. 134). Recently, excavations[61] have revealed a large building, presumably a palace, and a curious beehive-shaped structure which may have been an enormous silo. This was certainly an important town and brick scattered mounds attest the presence of other buildings.

Plates 7, 9

The remaining Meroitic sites all lie to the east of the river in the Island of Meroe. All across the western part of this area are the traces of settlement, but as already mentioned it seems that the eastern part stretching to the river Atbara was not occupied by the Meroites. They were primarily a people of the river, and it is noticeable that the 'inland' sites all lie along the great wadis, the Wadi Hawad, Wadi Awateib and Wadi el-Banat.

Only the most important sites can be described here.[62] Two of them are of exceptional importance: Naqa, in the Wadi Awateib, and Musawwarat es-Sofra, in the Wadi el-Banat. Both these sites lie at about one day's camel or donkey journey from the river, and their importance as staging points on trade routes to the east probably accounts for their position just as much as do the agricultural potentialities of the area.

Fig. 23. Plan of the temples at Naqa (after Budge)

Naqa lies on open ground in the Wadi Awateib and just over 20 miles from where the Wadi debouches into the Nile beside Wad ben Naqa. It comprises a number of temples, the remains of a town and two large cemeteries. The temples have been given different designations by different writers, the most convenient probably being that of Lepsius, which is used here. The best known and preserved are A and B. A is often known as the Lion Temple since it seems to have been dedicated to the Lion-god Apedemek. It has a very simple plan and its interest lies in the inscriptions and reliefs. It was built in the time of Netekamani and Amanitare, who are portrayed in the reliefs and their names given in Meroitic hieroglyphs in several places. It must therefore date from the very late first century BC or early first century AD.

The king and queen are shown on the two pylons at the entrance of the temple, destroying their enemies. They stand in attitudes derived from Egyptian originals, but showing char‑ acteristic Meroitic details of dress and personal adornment. It will be seen that the queen is distinctly plump, reflecting what must have been a local standard of beauty in marked contrast to Egyptian taste. The walls of the temple, both inside and out, show scenes of the king and queen, accompanied by Prince Arikhankharer worshipping various gods. The artistic con‑ ventions remain Egyptian with faces shown in profile with one startling exception, where on an inside wall a god is shown full‑face in a quite distinctive style obviously derived from Roman art.

Plate 8

Fig. 24

Fig. 25

The most interesting scene of all is that on the outside of the back wall where the royal trio, with the prince represented twice, stands before the Lion‑god, who is here uniquely shown with three heads and four arms, in a representation that sug‑ gests Indian influence.[63] In this scene the details of royal dress and decoration are clearly visible, and the tasselled cloaks worn by the king and queen are of particular interest, as are also the elaborate rings and beads. The details are well and carefully carved in these reliefs and even the neck wrinkles, still regarded as a sign of beauty in parts of Africa today, are indicated.

Plates 10, 11

Near by stands Temple B stylistically in marked contrast to the essentially Egyptian impression given by A. This remark‑ able little temple clearly owes much to classical influence, al‑ though containing Egyptian elements in the winged disk and frieze of cobra heads. It has no inscription, but it seems to date from about the time of Netekamani and may have been in‑ tended to form part of the approach to Temple A, though it is not in line with the main axis of that temple.

Plates 13, 14

Fig. 24.   Reliefs on the pylons of the Lion Temple, Naqa (after Budge)

The largest of the temples, though not well preserved, is
Temple D and the kiosk which lies in front of it. This temple
is contemporary with A and has the name of Netekamani and
Amanitare on the lintel of the main entrance, although in this

case they are shown with a different prince, Arikakhatani. An
avenue of stone rams led from the kiosk to the temple entrance. Plate 16

Temple F, lying to the east of the others, bears the name
of Queen Shanakdakhete; this is of some importance because, Plate 15

Fig. 25 A god depicted full-face, from an inside wall of the Lion Temple, Naqa (after Budge)

although the inscription accompanying the cartouche is in Egyptian, the royal name is in Meroitic hieroglyphs and is thus the first Meroitic inscription to which a date can be given.[64]

In addition to these buildings, all rising to some height, there are ruined remnants of at least two other temples. The site of the town can be identified, covering an area of nearly a square mile, where stone blocks, column drums, and fragments of red brick abound. There are two cemeteries both consisting of stone-covered mound graves. The only one so far opened belongs to the post-Meroitic period.[65]

Some ten miles to the north-east of Naqa, at the head of the Wadi el-Banat and in a natural basin five to six miles across and surrounded by hills, lies the site of Musawwarat es-Sofra. This site, the most remarkable and dramatic in the Sudan, is

Fig. 26

92

of considerable complexity and has always been something of an enigma; neither its date nor its purpose were clear prior to the recent work of the East German expedition.

The main feature, the 'Great Enclosure', consists of a number of buildings and walled enclosures surrounding a temple built on a platform, rather similar in lay-out to the Sun Temple at Meroe. On stylistic grounds, this central temple appears to be-long to the first century AD or a little earlier, but there are no inscriptions other than secondary graffiti, which are plentiful.

Plates 17, 18

Fig. 26.   Plan of Musawwarat es-Sofra (after Budge)

0 10 20 30 40 50 **Metres**

This temple is surrounded by a colonnade, some of whose columns have interesting reliefs. Outside the colonnaded temple is a series of corridors and ramps which connect the various parts of the complex, and which are not known from any other Meroitic site. The number of representations of elephants in the sculptures suggests that this animal played an important part at Musawwarat es-Sofra; the large enclosures may have been de-signed to herd them in, the ramps being for their convenience since they could more easily negotiate them than they could steps. It may be that here was a centre for the training of ele-phants for military and ceremonial purposes. The remarkable wall terminating in the figure of an elephant is unique and is further evidence of the importance of this animal.

The numerous graffiti are mainly in Meroitic, and a number seem to be invocations to the god Apedemek; but some are in other languages – one is in Egyptian demotic, one in Greek, and several in Old Nubian.[66] A Latin inscription, the most southerly known, was removed to Berlin by Lepsius.[67] East of this main temple lies another (North East Temple), approached by a ramp and with the main entrance flanked by two colossal statues.

The most remarkable discovery of the recent excavations[68] has been in the temple previously known as the 'South East Temple', but since re-named the 'Lion Temple'. Before ex-cavation, this building appeared as a pile of rubble in which only a few pieces of sculptured reliefs were visible, and was assumed to belong to a late period. Recent work has revealed the reliefs on the outside of the south wall which were found to be almost intact, since the wall had collapsed outwards and the blocks had been preserved by having lain face down in the sand. When the blocks were reassembled, inscriptions in Egyp-tian were found together with the name of King Arnekhamani.

These inscriptions, which provide valuable information about Meroitic religion, are also of great significance chrono-

Plate 20
Fig. 27

Fig. 4

Plate 19

Fig. 30

*Fig. 27. Relief show-
ing a king riding an
elephant, from Musaw-
warat es-Sofra*

logically.[69] The style of language as well as of the hieroglyphs
is early Ptolemaic in date and the excavator suggests that the
temple was built between 235 and 211 BC.[70]

Excavation was also carried out on two other smaller temples,
both probably of later date, on a workshop area and on a building
just south of the main enclosure. An investigation was made of
the great *hafir*,[71] a device for water storage, made by constructing
a large earth rampart with an opening in the direction of the
'run-off' of rain water from the hills. Such *hafirs* occur in a
number of places in the Island of Meroe and all seem to be of
Meroitic date.

Of other sites, a few only can be mentioned. Basa, lying in
the Wadi Hawad, has a temple and a *hafir*. The temple was
partly excavated by Crowfoot in 1907.[72] He found nine lion
statues there, four of them at the entrance to the temple, and
five standing round the *hafir*, as if to guard it. One of these has
the name of Amanikhabale on it and therefore dates from about
the middle of the first century BC. A large stone frog was also
found here,[73] but has not been traced in recent years. Umm
Usuda lies further east and consists of a *hafir*,[74] which also has
stone lions associated with it. In all it has seven lions and three

rams, together with a stela in Meroitic cursive. Its name, which is Arabic for 'mother of lions', presumably refers to the presence of these stone animals.

Further south at Jebel Qeili, close to the modern track which leads across the Butana from Khartoum to Kassala, an extremely interesting scene is carved on a large granite boulder at the foot of the hill. This scene, which is very difficult to see, had been visited and commented on by various writers[75] with only moderate success, until the East German expedition of 1958

Fig. 7

were able to take a latex impression from which the figure on an earlier page was made.[76] This, for the first time, allowed all the details of the scene to be studied, and showed that the previously undeciphered royal name was that of King Sherkarer who reigned early in the first century AD.

The scene is one of victory, with the king facing the Sun-god who holds a group of captured enemies by a cord hanging from his left hand. The king's dress is much as in other portrayals of Meroitic royalty, and, in addition to the bow and arrows held in his right hand, he has a sword hung from the left shoulder in the manner of the modern Beja as well as some of the Arab tribes of the eastern Butana today. The Sun-god is shown full face and holds in his right hand what appears to be a head of *sorghum,* still the standard grain crop of the central Sudan. The portrayal of the Sun-god shows a very marked similarity to a class of representations of a sun deity at Hatra and other West Asian sites, which are regarded as Parthian and date from the first two centuries AD. A most unusual feature is the realistic and lively portrayal of seven bodies of enemies falling down a hill, a scene without parallel from Meroitic times. This scene has been regarded as a commemoration of a victory over Axum but there is nothing specifically Axumite in the appearance of the enemies.

West of the Nile there are no attested Meroitic sites although it is highly likely that they are waiting to be found. In the middle of the Bayuda desert at Fura, a rectangular stone fort has produced a few Meroitic sherds.[77] It may well have been a staging point on the trans-Bayuda route mentioned by Nasta-sen in his inscription (see above, p. 38).

At Soba, on the Blue Nile fourteen miles up-stream from Khartoum, a stone ram of Meroitic date and familiar style was found, and is now to be seen in the grounds of the Anglican cathedral in Khartoum.[78] It has an inscription in Meroitic hieroglyphs with a broken cartouche giving the name of a king … reqerem not otherwise known,[79] but thought by Hintze to be buried in pyramid N. 30 at Meroe. From the style of the ram and the inscription, the proposed date (AD 165–184) seems rather late. No other traces of Meroitic occupation have been found there and it may be that the ram was removed from some other site at the time when Soba was the capital of a Christian state.

Further to the south, the only place to have produced identi-fiable Meroitic material is Sennar, but along the banks of the White Nile are a number of mounds containing pottery which resembles some of the African wares found at other Meroitic sites.[80] Sennar is the most southerly site of this culture so far known and, unless other evidence becomes available, must be considered to mark approximately the southern boundary of the state. The evidence is all from graves and no town has been discovered, but the richness of the material suggests that there must have been a settlement of some size and importance here. The grave contents, found whilst making the Sennar dam, have suffered considerable vicissitudes and a number of them were lost when the ship in which they were being sent to Eng-land sank in the Red Sea. The story has recently been told and the material given definitive publication[81]. The principal items discovered were a number of bronze bowls of well-known Meroitic type and presumably dating from the first two cen-turies BC.

Not far from Sennar lies the large cemetery of Jebel Moya, which, while not producing any certainly Meroitic material, seems to be contemporary. There has been considerable discus' sion of the date of this site, which has been summed up by Addison,[82] who concludes that, in spite of the presence of Napatan objects and marked local variations in the pottery, there is sufficient similarity to much Meroitic pottery to establish the site as of that period.

Meroitic bronze bowls have been found at Axum in Ethio' pia,[83] but they are probably objects carried there in trade rather than evidence for Meroitic occupation, and we have no know' ledge of commercial or political contacts between the two powers.

CHAPTER IV

Art

THE ART OF MEROE has never yet been the subject of detailed study and like many other aspects of the culture, has been passed over as a provincial aberration of Egyptian art containing some extraneous elements. This is not a fair judge-ment; Meroitic art has a flavour sufficiently distinctive to merit the consideration and description of its more important indi-vidual pieces.

The development of this art presents a number of problems of chronology and of outside influences for which there is still too little information to provide adequate answers. As an artis-tic expression of a separate culture, sufficiently independent to be considered apart from that of Egypt, it developed only in the latter part of the period we are considering. During the whole time of the rule of Meroe, from *c.* 590 BC to AD 300, distinc-tively Meroitic art is found only from about the third century BC onwards. Meroitic writing also seems to start at the same time and much of the material regarded as characteristic of Meroe is of an even later date, some of it not being earlier than the be-ginning of the first century AD.

The reasons for this are not yet discernible in the historical, nor even properly in the archaeological record, though we have already pointed out that Meroitic settlements in the northern part of the realm nearly all belong to the period after the birth of Christ. There seems to have been a very rapid transition, and a cultural break at this time has been suggested;[1] but until a stratified site with occupation from Napatan or at least early Meroitic times is found and excavated the reality of this break cannot be tested. Whatever the reality of this cultural and per-haps also linguistic change, the influence of Egypt remained very great and to the end of Meroitic times the art forms current in Egypt made themselves strongly felt.

The non-Egyptian and non-Mediterranean element in the art is more difficult to define and still remains largely unstudied. The lack of any indigenous material from immediately pre-Meroitic times makes it difficult to isolate specific influences of a non-northern character and nothing is known of the art, if any existed, of the peoples who inhabited this part of the Nile Valley in earlier times.

There is a strong hint of an eastern influence to be seen in some aspects of Meroitic art and these will be referred to as the objects themselves are described. The routes by which this eastern element came to the Nile are not certain but it must be assumed that the trans-Butana caravan trails to the Red Sea were the paths by which influences from Persia, India and perhaps further east came to Meroe. We know very little of the archaeology of the Red Sea coast at this time and no objects identifiable as Meroitic have been found there, but it is certain that ships were passing up and down the Red Sea in Hellenistic and Roman times and also that the harbour of Ptolemais Theron had been established as a trading post as early as the third century BC.

The residual influences can be regarded as native Meroitic and African and are shown as transforming the known artistic styles of other countries and areas to an art which is distinctive and characteristic of the period and culture and unmistakably Meroitic. This specific Meroitic element in the art is not easy to define – it can be seen in the well-rounded female figures, in the highly individual pottery styles, and in the use of motifs and subjects not familiar elsewhere. Amongst the favourite subjects of the Meroitic artists are elephants and lions, animals rarely seen in Egyptian art, and which are evidently an entirely local contribution. The lion, emblem of the important local god Ape-demek, is frequently shown on the reliefs as well as in sculpture

in the round and evidence as yet unpublished from Musawwarat es-Sofra suggests that lions were tamed and kept in the
temples as living representatives of the god. The elephant shown
many times in reliefs as well as in other representations was also
of great significance.[2] It seems to have been used for war as well
as for ceremonial purposes, and the knowledge of such use may
well have come from India. The African elephants used in
warfare in Ptolemaic and Roman times were almost certainly
trained by Meroites.

This obviously indigenous element might well be called
'African' and so in a sense it is, since Meroe is a part of Africa;
but the term is somewhat misleading since it suggests a relationship with art forms of sub-Saharan Africa as they are known
today, the art which springs most to mind when Africa is
mentioned. It is hard to find any connection between the art of
Meroe and that of parts further south, whether to east or west.
Attempts have been made to see Meroitic influence in the
famous bronze heads from Ife in Nigeria, but an objective study
discloses no artistic resemblance, and the distance in time and
space between Meroe and late medieval Nigeria, must cause
grave doubts to be cast on any suggestion of inter-relationship.

SCULPTURE

The art of Meroe is best known from a comparatively small
number of pieces of sculpture in the round and from the reliefs
on temples and pyramid chapels. The few examples of sculpture in the round all appear to be of royal persons or divine
figures. Few of them can be dated with precision; but most
appear to belong to the first century BC and the first AD.

A number of such figures were certainly made to stand at
the entrance to temples, and of these the best known are the
colossi at Hag Zummar on Argo Island (see p. 68). They
represent a royal figure and have been ascribed by Dunham to

Plate 23

Netekamani.[3] They are made of granite from the quarries at Tumbus just above the Third Cataract, which had been in use since at least Egyptian XVIII Dynasty times. Dunham has given a detailed description of these two statues as well as the argument for identifying them with Netekamani, and it need not be repeated here except to say that in default of any inscription on the statues the identification is made on stylistic grounds and by comparison of details of dress and ornament with those shown on the temple reliefs of Netekamani at Naqa.

The placing of statues at the entrance to temples seems to have been a common practice and examples are known from several other sites. At Musawwarat es-Sofra the North-east Temple has two much-decayed colossi from which little detail now remains. At Naqa two statues have been found which though not colossi may have been used in the same way; they also have been badly damaged but some details can be seen.[4] They represent male figures, presumably royal, and from such details of dress as survive they also seem to be of about the time of Netekamani. A fragment of a rather similar piece has recently been found at Meroe near to palace 750.

Meroe has produced a greater variety of statuary than any other site and shows a number of different styles, the most interesting pieces perhaps being those found in the ruins of the so-called Temple of Isis.[5] These figures seem to have been re-used as bases for columns of a later temple, but it can be assumed that they also stood on either side of a temple entrance. They have usually been described as being of a king and a queen following the excavator's original description. There is nothing in the so-called queen's statue to suggest that it is of a female; indeed, it is certain that each represents a male royal figure. Garstang says that the female (*sic*) figure was painted black, but today it bears no trace of colour.[6] Dating of these figures presents some difficulties. There are several points of resemblance to the regalia of Netekamani in the shoulder straps and the large ball

Plate 19

Plate 21

Plate 24

beads seen on the 'queen' and the kilt also has analogies at this period, but the whole appearance of the two statues is much heavier and cruder than the Argo statues or the Naqa temple reliefs. There are differences in detail between the two statues but from the place of their finding and the general similarity it seems reasonable to assume that they are contemporary. In view of the decline in artistic skill shown, they are presumably post-Netekamani and can be tentatively placed in the second century AD.

Other pieces from Meroe included a number from the 'Roman bath', such as the reclining man, all showing strong Mediterranean influence. Many of these pieces are of plaster, as are also the two remarkable statues of a man and woman found in palace No. 295 close to the bath. Amongst other statues found there are three figures, playing musical instruments; two of these, one playing pipes and the other a harp are still in *situ*; the third, playing *auloi,* has only recently come to light,[7] but in the absence of information on associated material more exact dating is impossible. These are interesting as showing that music played a part in Meroitic life and the discovery of actual *auloi* in at least two places[8] is confirmation of this.

In addition to sculptured representations of the human form there were many examples of carved stone rams flanking avenues leading to temples, as at Meroe before the temple of Amun, and at Naqa; also from Meroe are a number of small lions in sandstone, and there is the larger lion figure from Basa.

Together with these mainly life-size or more than life-size statues there must also have been a class of smaller pieces, though very few have been preserved. One of them, showing a king, found in the Lion Temple at Meroe and made of steatite, is worth noting.[9] It shows much of the usual regalia, including the large beads and the bracelets on the upper arm, but also has, uniquely, an amulet which seems to represent a shrine hanging on the chest and suspended from a chain round the neck. The

Plate 25

Plates 26, 27

Plate 16

Plate 37

Ba-statues, which were placed on tombs, provide some quite good examples of sculpture of the human face and one from Faras in sandstone is a pleasing example of this type.

Sculpture in bronze is less common but a number of small pieces were found at Kawa, amongst them two of special im-portance. One of these came from Temple T at Kawa and Plates 34, 35 represents a king or a god, possibly Atum. It is a delicately made piece and shows the characteristic royal trappings com-mon in representations of kings in the first century BC. It may be of about that date. The other piece is the head of a goddess; Plate 36 it is hollow and has a square socket within as though it were intended to be fixed to a wooden post – perhaps to the prow of a ceremonial boat. The importance of this piece lies in the car-touche of King Arnekhamani incised on the front. The cutting of the hieroglyphs is of poorer workmanship than that of the head itself, which is well done, and this suggests that they were a later addition. The style is Ptolemaic, but although of Egyp-tian style the emphasis on the neck wrinkles strongly suggests Meroitic manufacture.

Of pieces known to be of foreign make and imported to Meroe, the most famous is the bronze head of Augustus the Plate 28 finding of which has already been described. Two Hellenistic bronze heads came from pyramid Beg. N. 5, both from statues now lost, and represent the god Dionysus. They are certainly of Plate 38 Greek workmanship, but cannot be dated very precisely since similar pieces were made from the fourth century BC to about the middle of the first century AD.[10] An unusual piece is a small bronze figure of a camel, the only representation of this animal known from Meroitic times, from pyramid Beg. N. 5. of the early first century AD. Vercoutter[11] has suggested that it may be of Chinese origin.

This is perhaps the place to mention the unique gold stat-uette of a queen found by chance at Jebel Barkal. This is one of the most remarkable of the smaller pieces of statuary and the only one known in this material.[12] On stylistic grounds it can be dated to the first century BC. It conveys a suggestion of the Greek archaistic figures which were popular at that time and which gave rise to the depictions of Athena on some coins of the Indian frontier.[13] Although damaged by the finders, most of the detail is well preserved and shows the characteristic royal dress and adornments. The nearest analogies to these details are to be seen in the Naqa reliefs, and it may be that this statuette represents Queen Amanitare.[13a]

Plates 29, 30

Before passing on to a consideration of temple reliefs, reference may be made to three small pieces of relief work, all probably from Meroe. One, of dark red slate, comes from the Lion Temple; originally one piece with scenes on the two sides, it was split anciently into two.[14] It shows on the one side King Tanyidamani in full regalia wearing the long quilted or embroidered(?) garment known from Naqa statues and temple reliefs, and on the other the Lion-god, Apedemek. The second piece from the Amun Temple shows a scene of a king and a queen making offerings, the king to Amun and the queen to Isis. The very fragmentary Meroitic text does not help in the identification, nor is the king's name given. The work is crude by comparison with the former piece, suggesting that it is later in date, and the form of the letters in the inscription would make some time in the first century AD probable. The third fragment is a sandstone plaque which is thought to have come from Meroe.[15] It shows Prince Arikhankharer, whose name is written in Meroitic hieroglyphs in a cartouche at top left, smiting his enemies in conventional style. Between the prince's feet a dog savages one of the enemies; this dog is carved in Roman style and Griffith considered that it could not be earlier than the second quarter of the second century AD.[16] Behind is a very unusual portrayal of a winged goddess, to which no exact parallel is known, but which shows what may be Persian influence.

Plate 31

Plate 32

Plate 33

Reliefs on the temples and chapels are found in profusion and provide the best material for assessing the changes in Me⁄ roitic art, as well as giving valuable information about icono⁄ graphy and religion and on details of royal dress and regalia. The largest group is to be found on the walls of the chapels belonging to the pyramids at Meroe, and there are fragmentary remains at the Barkal pyramids and at Nuri. Other important reliefs are to be found on the Lion Temple at Naqa and the recently excavated Lion Temple at Musawwarat. All the reliefs are profoundly influenced by Egyptian artistic and religious ideas. Even the very latest ones such as that of the chapel of Begarawiya N. 36, which appears to date from some time in the third century AD, still represent the same familiar scenes of a seated king with processions approaching him.

There are virtually no reliefs earlier than those of the first pyramid chapels at Meroe, of the late fourth century BC. Some of the chapels at Nuri may have had reliefs, and very small fragments are observable at the pyramids of Amaniastabarqa (Nu. 2), Harsiotef (Nu. 13), and Nastasen (Nu. 15), but it seems that up to and including Baskakaren chapel decoration of any sort was the exception. From about this time onwards it becomes the rule, and even quite minor tombs have decorations of this kind.

There remain in a usable state of preservation virtually only the Meroe reliefs, and we have therefore material only from the full Meroitic period, with very little to indicate development from Napatan times. But at Meroe itself enough is preserved for us to observe stylistic changes over a period of about 600 years.

The main decoration on the walls at all periods is a scene of the ruler seated on a throne, of which the arm⁄rests are in most cases in the shape of a lion. The goddess Isis stands protectively behind the ruler, and on occasion other members of the royal family stand behind her. The early tombs in the series have

Fig. 28

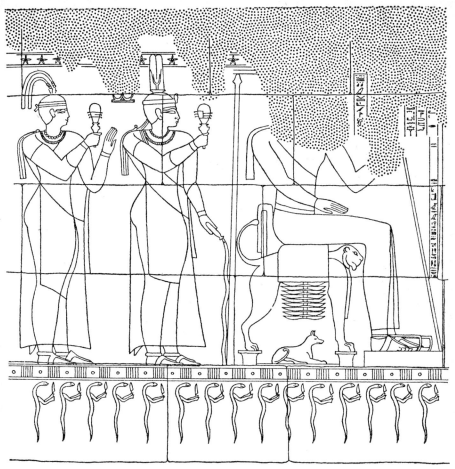

Fig. 28. Relief from the pyramid chapel of Arqamani, Beg. N. 7 (after Dunham)

reliefs in a good Hellenistic Egyptian style, particularly marked
in the case of Arqamani who was buried in tomb Beg. N. 7,
where the Egyptian character is so strong as to suggest that the
craftsmen were themselves Egyptian. Of these earlier tombs, the
best preserved reliefs are those of tomb Beg. N. 11, assumed on
rather scanty evidence to be the tomb of either Queen Nahirqa

Fig. 29

107

– her name occurs on pyramid Beg. N. 8 as the wife of a king whose name has not survived – or of Shanakhdakhete who is known to have been a queen from an inscription in Temple F at Naqa.[17] Whoever these reliefs may commemorate they are of considerable interest; they contain more detail than most, and here for the first time is shown a procession of small figures bearing palm branches, a scene which becomes common and appears in nearly all chapel reliefs from this time (early second century BC) on.

With pyramid N. 12 – and archaeological considerations make it clear that this dates from about the same time as N. 11 – we begin to find full Meroitic royal regalia depicted. It is shown in considerable detail, is markedly different from the Egyptian-ized regalia of the earlier tombs, and seems to mark some im-portant cultural change. It was of considerable complexity, and it covers a wide range of style of dress and personal adornment. Yet certain common features can be recognised, such as the large beads which are nearly always worn, the fringed garment draped over the right shoulder and the tassels which hang from the shoulders. There is a variety of head-dress, most of it derived from Egypt, but a close-fitting cap tied with a fillet is the most common wear.

The subject matter of the reliefs on the Sun Temple has al-ready been described (page 81); they are, however, of special interest artistically since they are the only examples of reliefs showing scenes other than the very formalised processions of gods and royalties. They have a freedom and vigour in marked contrast to the stylised reliefs from the pyramid chapels and other temples, and give details of weapons and equipment which are not available from other sources. In view of the ab-sence of comparative material it is very difficult to date the main scenes, though they do not appear to be very late and could be as early as the time of Aspelta. On the other hand some of the reliefs on the west wall, which are in quite a different style,

Fig. 29. Relief from the pyramid chapel of Nahirqa, Beg. N. 11 (after Dunham)

particularly the scene of two horsemen, strongly suggest Roman influence.

The other most important reliefs are at Musawwarat es-Sofra and Naqa. The earliest ones, perhaps the first true Meroitic reliefs, are those at Musawwarat es-Sofra, where the finding of the walls of the 'Lion Temple' in a very well-preserved state has given us valuable material for chronology (p. 40) as well as for artistic development. These reliefs, of King Arnekhamani, *Fig. 30* are of early Ptolemaic style, as not only the treatment of the figures but also the hieroglyphs and the language of the inscriptions show. There are, however, Meroitic elements to be seen in the adornment of the royal figure and in the unique repre-*Fig. 31* sentation of thumb rings on the right hand of both the king and the Lion-god Apedemek on the north wall. These thumb rings, known in some numbers from Meroitic sites, have been something of a mystery; they used to be described as mace or staff heads, and possibly some were used in this way, but Arkell's discovery in a Meroitic cemetery at Khartoum[18] of two *in situ* on the right thumbs of skeletons showed that they were sometimes so worn. Their purpose has been argued for some while,[19] but Arkell's view that they were used as archer's draw

Fig. 30. Restored reliefs from the south and north walls of the Lion Temple, Musawwarat es-Sofra (after Hintze)

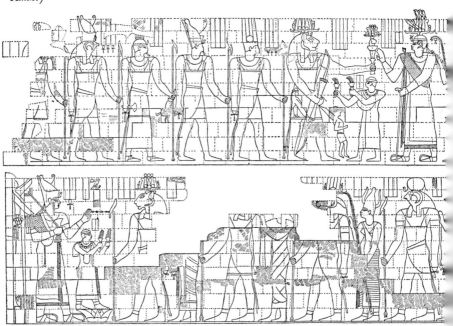

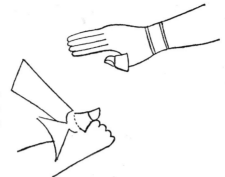

Fig. 31. Thumb rings on the hands of a god and a king, Lion Temple, Musawwarat es-Sofra (after Hintze)

rings has been generally accepted. The Musawwarat es-Sofra relief lends some support to this view; though the ring worn by the king may have been purely ornamental, it is perhaps significant that Apedemek has a ring on the thumb of his right hand which also holds a bow and quiver, and this suggests that all three are associated.

Fig. 32

Apart from the Lion Temple reliefs, the other sculpture at this site is restricted to some of the columns and their capitals. The style of this sculpture is quite different from anything else known in Meroitic art and in its high relief as well as in some of the figures, it is reminiscent of Indian art of the early centuries AD. More representations of elephants have been found here recently and some of the columns have elephants and lions carved at the base as supports, another hint of Indian influence.

The sculptured scenes from Naqa, dating from the beginning of the first century AD, are probably the best-known of all Meroitic reliefs. The most important ones are to be found on the walls of Temple A, also known as the Lion Temple, and a description of them has already been given (p. 88). About three hundred years later than similar scenes on the Musawwa-rat es-Sofra Lion Temple, they show how little the main ele-ments in Meroitic art had changed during that time although the workmanship had declined. There are differences in detail in the royal regalia and dress, but the over-all impression makes

Fig. 32.
Thumb ring
(after Dunham)

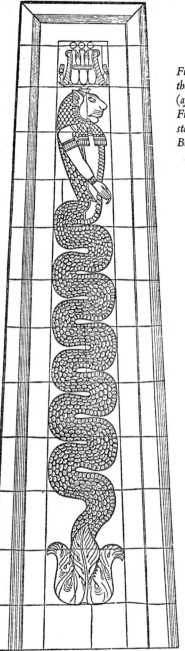

Fig. 33. Lion-god with the body of a snake, Naqa (after Budge)

Fig. 34. Lion-god's standard, Naqa (after Budge)

it clear that the Meroitic royal line has retained the same artistic ideas over the centuries. The new element is to be seen in the representation of the Lion-god with multiple head and arms and in the occasional evidence of influence from the Classical world as in the full-face head of the god here illustrated. The pylons of this temple carry a fine representation of the king and queen smiting their enemies, a motif which goes back to Egyptian New Kingdom times, though the treatment by the Meroitic artist shows considerable differences. On the side walls of these pylons is a remarkable relief of the Lion-god shown with the body of a snake and emerging from a lotus; this again has a strong suggestion of Indian influence. So strong indeed is this hint of Indian artistic elements in some of the art of Meroe, that it has led Vercoutter to say that he considers Meroitic art to be 'tout aussi indianisant qu'égyptisant'.[20]

Fig. 25

Fig. 24

Plate 12

Fig. 33

Among the less distinguished pieces of sculptured stone relief must be mentioned the offering tables. These have been found in great quantity in the cemeteries and are of considerable value for the study of the Meroitic language since they frequently bear a prayer formula and the name of the deceased (see Chapter VI)

Figs. 35, 36

Figs. 35, 36. Meroitic offering tables (after Budge and Griffith)

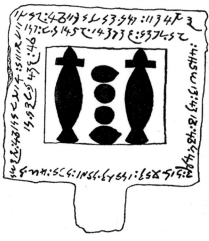

written round the edge. They are usually roughly sculptured in very shallow relief and often show a scene of the god Anubis and the goddess Nephthys pouring a libation before, or some/times onto, a table which carried a representation of food offer/ings. Other examples do not have the divine figures but show only offerings of food and drink.

POTTERY

The pottery is the best/known of all the artistic products of Meroitic civilization. It occurs in profusion at many sites and has figured prominently in a number of publications.[21] This pottery owes its fame not only to the quantity in which it has been found but also to its high quality. It ranks with the finest products of ceramic art of the ancient world both in the quality

Fig. 37.   Meroitic pottery : fine ware

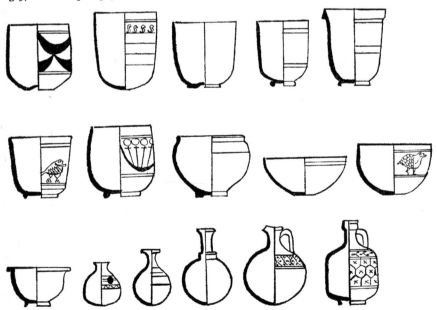

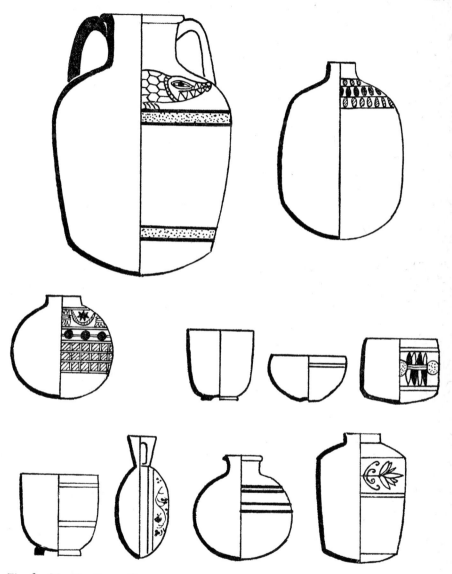

Fig. 38.   Meroitic pottery: utility ware

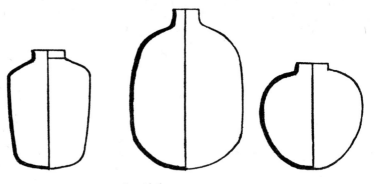

Fig. 39. Meroitic pottery: burnished ware

of its fabric and the style of its decoration, and, together with the later and related pottery of Christian Nubia,[22] forms the main contribution of the ancient Sudan to the artistic heritage of the Nile Valley.

The two constant elements in Meroitic culture are well exemplified in this pottery where there is a clear distinction between the Mediterranean and the African traditions, and where both styles are found in contemporary association. There is also a functional significance in these two styles, and throughout the history of Kush it can be observed that there were at nearly all times two quite different traditions – the wheel-turned wares of northern inspiration made by the men, and the hand-made wares which are the work of women. The wheel-made pottery has shown wide variations and responses to stylistic changes, whilst the women's pottery has shown a remarkable continuity of form and style. Women's pottery reflects a deep-rooted African tradition and it is still made to-day in what is recognizably the same style, not only in the Sudan but in many other parts of Africa.

Until recently the published collections have all been from cemeteries, and with the exception of Meroe itself, all from sites in Lower Nubia. As a result of this, very little is known of the pottery from the southern part of the Meroitic state, and as the occupation of Lower Nubia was confined to the period from the third century BC onwards the earlier pottery is virtually unknown. It is only recently that a properly detailed analysis and classification has been made of Meroitic pottery and this study by Adams[23] supersedes the more superficial ones made by earlier workers, and must be regarded as standard until more evidence has been gained from stratified sites.

By studying the pottery from the northern part of the Meroitic state, both from cemeteries and from a small number of dwelling sites, Adams has reduced the vast quantity of material and the various classifications previously made to some order, and through his own excavations of stratified sites has been able to establish the beginnings of a chronology. The only previously attempted chronology for this pottery was that based on Griffith's ordering of the graves at Faras, and this has always been seen to be unsatisfactory since the same pottery wares were found in all the types of graves, except for very late ones of post-Meroitic times.

In Adams' classification the pottery falls into five main groups which he calls: I, Meroitic Fine; II, Meroitic Utility; III, Meroitic Burnished; IV, Imported Graeco-Roman; V, Meroitic Domestic. Groups I, II and III represent the Mediterranean style of wheel-made pottery, IV is all imported, much of it from Egypt but some from further afield, whilst V is the hand-made pottery of African tradition.

These five groups are subdivided into a number of wares; they can conveniently be studied in Adams' paper[24] and we need only concern ourselves with the over-all characteristics. In figures 37–41 typical pot forms from the different groups are shown. Group I contains the well-known fine wares, frequently painted with a variety of patterns such as those in the figure overleaf, as well as zoomorphic designs. Sometimes they are decorated with bands of stamped decorations. The vessels of this ware are all small and the fabric of the pots is fine and

Figs. 37–41

Plates 34–43

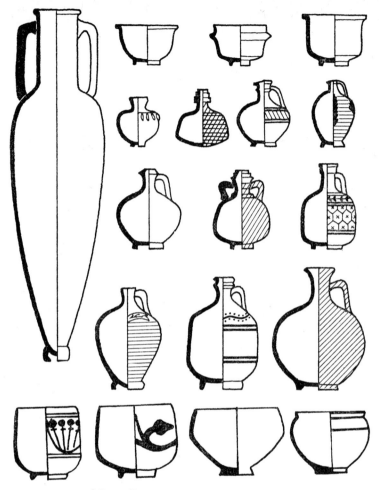

Fig. 40. Imported Graeco-Roman pottery

delicate. This pottery style occurs amongst the earliest Meroitic
levels in Lower Nubia and presents something of an artistic
and chronological problem since it appears to have no clear
forerunners. Appearing suddenly in the late fourth or early third
centuries BC as a fully developed ceramic art, whose decline but

not its origin can be seen, it remains a mystery. Whatever its origins may be, the pottery has a marked character of its own, though in many cases the motifs hark back to Pharaonic Egypt, as in the uraei and the lotus design illustrated. These painted wares, in the words of Charleston, 'reveal an adaptation of Graeco-Roman formulae in which classical correctness gives way before the urgency of a bold and rhythmic brush work or the compulsion of an indigenous feeling for form',[25] and they are a delightful and important contribution to ceramic history.

Fig. 42

Fig. 41. Meroitic pottery: domestic ware

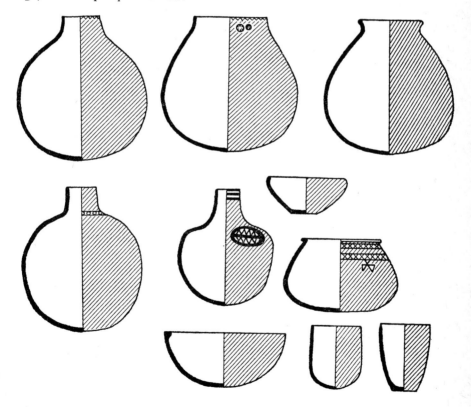

Plates 44–48

Ware Groups II and III represent coarser varieties of locally-made pottery and most of the vessels are larger than those of Group I. They are in the same tradition, their origins must be the same, and similar motifs and animal and human scenes are frequently found in the painted decoration. Some of the painted scenes are most elaborate as in the pot illustrated, where a man Plate 46 of African appearance is being eaten by a lion. Though the finer wares of Group I seem not to continue in manufacture right through the Meroitic period but to die out perhaps to-wards the end of the first century AD, their rather coarser equi-valents continue in use, some examples being found right at the end of Meroitic times.

The imported wares of Group IV are distinguished from the native pottery by their hard pink fabric, and show by their form and decoration that they came from areas under the influence of the Roman pottery tradition. They were presumably mostly made in Egypt as provincial copies of metropolitan wares but some of the better pieces may have come from parts of the Roman Empire nearer to Rome. They consist of a variety of Fig. 40 forms of which examples are shown on a previous page. With the exception of the amphorae which were extremely common in all habitation sites, most of the vessels of this ware are small. The majority of pots of the group are not painted though they frequently have a pink, cream, or red slip. One class is an Plates 53, 54 imitation of Roman barbotine ware with applied decoration of lumps and ridges. This sometimes takes flowing forms, and is reminiscent of British Castor ware of the second and third centuries AD though the Meroitic examples may be of the first century;[26] but the designs on the pots shown in the next two Plates are more common. There is too a class of red burnished pottery, probably also made in Egypt, which is an inferior copy Plate 43 (centre) of Roman Arretine ware. An example of this is the bowl from Faras. Some genuinely Italian, or at least European, pieces have been found both at Meroe and Wad ben Naqa. Of imported

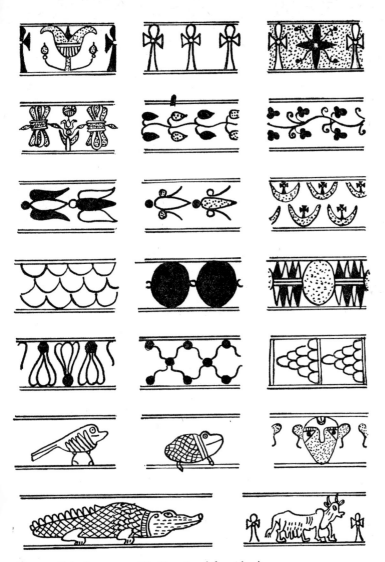

Fig. 42. Painted patterns on Meroitic pottery (after Adams)

pottery, though not falling into this group, the most important piece is the splendid Attic rhyton found in tomb S. 24 at Meroe. This piece which bears the name of the potter Sotades forms a valuable *terminus post quem* for this tomb, since Sotades is known to have been working in Athens in the latter fifth century BC and the rhyton dates from about 400 BC.[27]

The pottery of Group V is quite different from all the other wares. It is distinguished from them by a difference in tech-nique, since it is built up by hand and never made on the wheel,

Plates 57–59

and also by a different fabric composed of porous Nile mud and containing many small pieces of mica and an abundance of chopped straw and grass fragments. It is much softer than the other wares and was certainly fired at much lower temper-atures, probably not in kilns as with the more sophisticated pottery, but in the simple way still in use today – the pots are placed in a shallow hole in the ground, and dung and other inflammable material then piled on top and set alight.[28] This pottery is normally black, and the smaller vessels are often highly burnished; occasionally a burnished red slip has been applied. It is frequently decorated with incised patterns, some-

Plate 55

times filled with white, or, more rarely, red pigment. The shapes are based on gourds and bags, the normal containers over much of Africa, and in most parts the forerunners of pottery, and still used by nomads since they are less easily broken. Exceptionally, some of the small bowls reflect the shapes of metal vessels.

JEWELLERY AND PERSONAL ADORNMENT

The jewellery, known in the main from the royal tombs, is one of the finest products of Meroitic culture. It has been found in considerable quantity, the largest group being that discovered or acquired by Ferlini (see p. 27) and stated by him to have been found in pyramid N. 6 at Meroe, that of Queen Ama-nishakhete. There is some doubt as to the accuracy of Ferlini's

Fig. 43. Gold plaques
with names of Amtalqa and
Malenaqen from Meroe

story, and Budge, for one, believed that even if the jewellery did
come originally from Meroe it was not all from one pyramid
and was perhaps bought from a dealer.[29] Budge's scepticism
was not unwarranted, and earlier scholars had thrown doubt
on the genuineness of the material. Now that we know more of
Meroitic jewellery, there can be little doubt that this fine collection is genuine and is almost certainly from some of the royal
tombs at Meroe.[30]

It is perhaps safer to confine ourselves to certainly established
material from Reisner's excavations, which provides an array
of splendid jewellery. There is not a great deal of material from
the earlier Meroitic period and it only becomes plentiful and
rich in the first century BC. From such early examples as do
exist, from Nuri and the earlier Meroe burials, we can see that
the jewellery was closely modelled on contemporary Egyptian
styles and it is only in the later examples that it shows a specifically Meroitic character. Of the earlier pieces the gold plaques
from Meroe bearing the names of Amtalqa and Malenaqen call
for special notice. They formed part of a foundation deposit in
building No. 294, and are important evidence for early Meroitic occupation at Meroe. Their exact purpose is not known
though they may have been part of a necklace, the plaques being
originally strung together, with round beads of amethyst between them.

Fig. 43

Much of the jewellery is shown in use on the reliefs of queens, who can be seen to be wearing ornaments of all kinds in great profusion. Most of this jewellery was of gold and consisted of ear-rings, bracelets, and finger rings, often made up with semi-precious stones of which carnelian is the most common. I have chosen for illustration a group of earrings and bracelets of gold and carnelian from Meroe pyramid W. 5.

Plate 60, *Fig. 44*

This, and more, was found on the chest of a woman's corpse in the same burial chamber as another which is known from the chapel reliefs to have been that of a queen. The suggestion is that this subsidiary body was that of a maid-servant who had charge of her mistress's jewellery and that it was originally placed on her chest in a cloth or leather bag which has completely disintegrated. This group would appear to date from the end of the first century BC.

Fig. 44. Gold ear-rings from Meroe

All the gold work owes much to the example of Hellenistic Egyptian craftsmanship, but it has been too little studied to allow of detailed comment at present, or for changes in styles at different periods to be distinguished. It is likely that most of the pieces were made locally, and the quantity found is testimony to the wealth in gold of the Meroitic state. The designs of the jewellery show considerable variation though a Hathor head is a common element in the ear-rings. Flies, cowrie shells, and rams' heads are common as amulets, and the rings, both of gold and silver, show a considerable variety of engraved designs, many of which are of Egyptian inspiration and show figures of gods (Isis is common) as well as other Egyptian symbols. Some bearing Greek and other designs were imported, for example, one with the Greek inscription, XAPIC, and another with a figure of Athena holding a Victory in her hand.

Plate 62

Plate 61, *Fig. 45*

Fig. 45. Gold and silver rings from Meroe

Fig. 46. Silver plaques of lion's head from Meroe pyramids

A number of small silver plaques with lions and lions' heads depicted on them and pierced for attachment were found in pyramids Beg. N. 16 and N. 11 and are mentioned here as being decorative elements in precious metal. They may well have been attached to leather garments, such as a corselet, but are just as likely to have been decorations on horse trappings.

Fig. 46

Like the jewellery, beads are known in profusion from the cemeteries, but again little has been done to study changes of fashion and style during the many centuries they were in use.

The earlier burials produced beads of Egyptian style and a great many of the small faience amulets so well known from Egypt. One of the finest groups of these early beads dates from

Fig. 47

Fig. 47. Selection of faience amulets

the very beginning of our period and was found in pyramid Nu. 8, that of Aspelta. It consisted of eight rows of gold and beryl[31] beads, and one row made from amethysts.[32]

The richest and most varied beads date from later times and the best assortment comes from the Faras cemeteries. In addition to the common semi-precious stones, glass becomes an important material and a considerable number of such beads of Roman type were imported from Egypt. These include 'face beads' as well as some of millefiore glass. Of local materials, ostrich egg shell, in use from Neolithic times, continued to be commonly used, and the disc beads do not differ from those of earlier times. Globular and barrel-shaped beads of carnelian are frequently found, and by the first century BC pendants of the same material and of quartz came into use. Droplet beads of opaque quartz are characteristic of the very end of Meroitic times and are also common in the succeeding X-Group period.

Plate 63

METAL WARE

Since the only non-royal cemeteries so far to have been excavated are all of the third century BC or later, we have no information on non-royal metal objects of earlier times. But from this later period the greater part of the locally-made pieces consist of bronze bowls of simple style with a variety of incised decoration. These have been found in great number at Faras[33] as well as in other cemeteries as far south as Sennar.[34] It seems likely that the bowls with their characteristic Meroitic ornament were made in the country, though, since there are no natural occurrences of copper ore in the Nile Valley, the raw material must have been obtained from abroad.

Plates 64, 65

There are more elaborate shapes such as the bottle, probably dating from the first or second century AD, from Faras, and the footed bowl with two handles of about the same date from Gemai. A variety of bowls with handles for suspension have

Plate 68

Plate 66

Fig. 48. Scene showing elephants engraved on a bronze beaker from Meroe (after Dunham)

also been found of which some of the best examples were also from the Gemai cemetery[35] and are again of the first two centuries BC.

An unusual piece which almost certainly comes from Meroe[36] is a beaker with an incised scene of two elephants who are holding what seem to be a number of rings in their trunks. Above the head of one of them is an emblem which may be an owner's or maker's mark. A bowl from Karanog shows a scene of village and pastoral life.[37]

Fig. 48

Fig. 3

An unusual piece of bronze work is a cone-shaped object from Kawa which may have been a finial on a flag-staff. It bears the name of Amanikhabale and is therefore presumably of the first century BC.

The majority of the imported luxury objects that have survived are of metal, both bronze and silver, and a great many such pieces are known. Amongst the most common objects of Mediterranean origin are the lamps. Two specially fine examples were found in pyramid N.18 at Meroe, in which was

Plates 70, 72

Plate 73

Plate 71

Plate 69

Fig. 49

buried Queen Amanikhatashan who is dated to the latter part of the first century AD. These two lamps, with the handle in the form of the forepart of a centaur and that of a horse respectively, have not been closely dated, but their appearance suggests that they were made by Greek craftsmen within a hundred years of either side of the beginning of the present era. Two further lamps are illustrated, one from Faras of typical Roman shape, the other from a tomb in the West Cemetery at Meroe which is dated to the third century AD. This lamp with its decoration of two elephants' heads is another example of Meroitic devotion to this animal.

The last of the lamps shown is unusual. Found in pyramid N. 29 at Meroe, that of King Takideamani, it is of bronze but had an iron stem to which was fixed a bronze hook for sus-pension. The iron had decayed anciently but has been restored. The interest of this lamp is that, though of classical style with acanthus-shaped flame-guard and griffon's head hook, it ap-pears to be unique and no exact parallels are known.[38] It bears an inscription in Meroitic, to be read *abrilkheli she,* possibly the name of the maker, and in relief on the body of the lamp, in front of the filling-hole, is an emblem which occurs on other objects in the royal tombs and which Dunham[39] proposes should be regarded as a heraldic device indicating that it was intended for royal funeral equipment. Dunham also suggests that this is evidence that the lamp was made at Meroe itself.

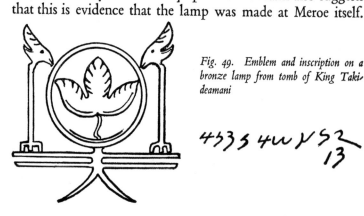

Fig. 49. *Emblem and inscription on a bronze lamp from tomb of King Taki-deamani*

*Fig. 50.   Engraving of a cow on a bronze bell
from Meroe pyramid N. 15*

If so, it indicates a high standard of local technical competence, or the presence of foreign artists in the town.

The hanging bowl in the shape of a boy's head is from Faras. Plate 77 The bowl and the handle are of bronze, the rings for attach- ment, originally of iron, have been restored and the eyes are inlaid in silver. It seems to date from the second or third century AD. Many other fine imported bronze objects are known but cannot be dealt with here, except for the splendid mirror-case from Faras. This case has on its outer side a female head and Plates 75, 76 shoulders of Hellenistic type whilst inside it is decorated with an engraved scene of Harpocrates seated on a lotus surrounded by nine creatures, some of them animals and birds, some purely mythical.

Bronze bells are also commonly found, many of them with incised scenes. Some of these are octagonal in shape with scenes of bound captives, others are of more conventional type – one from pyramid Beg. N. 29 has an elaborate scene of vultures attacking the slain. Some of these were used as cow-bells, as can be seen from the small example from Beg. N. 15 which Fig. 50 shows a cow wearing a bell of this type. A cow on the Karanog bowl (see page 127) also wears such a bell.

A certain number of silver vessels were also imported; of these the most remarkable is the goblet, originally gilded, found Plate 78 amongst the fallen blocks of pyramid Beg. N. 2. It cannot have been part of the contents of this tomb and was probably dropped

Plate 74

by plunderers. It appears to be Roman work and is likely to date from the middle of the first century AD. A silver porringer from Beg. N. 18 is another beautiful piece of about the same date. It has two designs scratched on it not dissimilar from those on the elephant beaker and the lamp described above, and perhaps also owner's marks.

GLASS

Because of their fragile nature, comparatively few complete glass vessels have survived, though fragments are common. All the pieces found are of Roman type, and there is nothing to suggest a local style or variation. This led the excavators of Karanog, where the finest examples of glass ware of the period were found, to state that 'vessels of blown glass were not manufac-tured in Nubia',[40] a view that is not invalidated by more recent investigations. This is not to say that glass making was un-known to the Meroites, but it seems that the only local use of glass was in the manufacture of beads.

We do not find any early pieces and we know that glass was comparatively rare in Egypt after the XVIII Dynasty until the beginning of the fourth century BC;[41] it was only after the im-portant technical change from moulded to blown glass at the beginning of the Christian era that it became at all common. Even then it was not plentiful until half-way through the first century AD,[42] and Karanis, which seems to have been the main manufacturing centre of Egypt and from which many pieces found in a Meroitic context probably came, was not in full production before about AD 100.

Plate 83

One fine moulded piece is known; it comes from Faras and was found in a grave dated to the first or second century AD.[43] Other vessels are nearly all of blown glass[44] and are mostly of the shapes used for containing unguents and oils. It is likely that in most cases they were imported more as containers for these valued materials than for their intrinsic beauty. One of the flasks illustrated is of green glass and comes from Faras; the type[45] is found all over the Roman world, and dates from the mid third to fourth century. A number of similar examples were found at Karanog. In addition to these two-handled flasks, many fragments of toilet bottles or *unguentaria* were found as well as a few complete ones. This is one of the commonest and most widespread of all Roman glass shapes[46] and having remained virtually the same from the first to the fifth century AD,[47] is of little help for close dating. Eight examples, made of green glass, came from pyramid Beg. N. 18. They were found, three in a fragmented state, in the remains of a wooden box which had been specially made to hold them, and in which they prob-ably travelled from Egypt.[48]

Plate 82

My final plate shows a two-coloured bottle;[49] it is of brown to purple glass with a decoration of yellow glass threads. It came from grave No. 300 at Meroe; being associated with pottery of very late or even post-Meroitic type,[50] it is itself to be dated between AD 200–400.

Plate 84

The examples of Meroitic art here described and illustrated give a tantalising hint of the richness of the culture, and of the wide variety of foreign influences at work. They provide a better clue to the importance of Meroe than does the fragmentary historical record.

CHAPTER V

The Language

ALTHOUGH IT IS now more than fifty years since Meroitic writing was first deciphered, the language still remains a mystery, and the meaning of its words still largely eludes us. This is a great barrier to a complete understanding of Meroitic history and culture, and until this language has been successfully read and the inscriptions translated, much of the story of Meroe will remain unknown.

Inscriptions in Meroitic have been known since 1819, when Gau published a few lines of *graffiti* from the temple at Dakka.[1] A few more were published in the early part of the nineteenth century, but they aroused little interest or comment until Lepsius made the first large collection in 1843–44. Lepsius, together with most of the early students of these texts, assumed that, when read, they would prove to be in Nubian, the language still spoken along the river from Diraw in Egypt to Debba a short way down-stream from the Fourth Cataract.[2] Lepsius himself later abandoned this view, coming to the conclusion that the language was related to Beja, spoken in the Red Sea Hills; while others held to the view that it was Nubian.

The credit for first reading the texts belongs to Griffith and by 1909[3] he had managed to establish the phonetic values of most of the signs. It then became clear that Meroitic was neither Nubian nor Beja. Some analogies with Nubian were seen, and though the few words apparently common to both languages could be accounted for by borrowing, Griffith commented that these 'analogies to Nubian both in structure and vocabulary are sufficiently striking to be worth mention'. But the language was not Nubian and what it is, or what relation it has to any of the other languages of Africa, still remains a mystery.

Spasmodic attempts have been made to find related languages, and in 1930 Zyhlarz reverted to the idea that the answer was to be found in a study of the Kushitic languages of the Red Sea littoral, the group to which Beja belongs.[4] His conclusions have been severely criticized by Hintze,[5] who showed that the two languages were not related; but Hintze was unable to make any positive suggestion. By 1955 Greenberg was forced to the conclusion that 'the language does not appear to be related to any existing language of Africa.[6] Though there is still very little evidence to go on, the increase in our knowledge of African linguistics since then has enabled us to make some progress.

The geographical distribution of the eastern Sudanic languages, to which Nubian and the Nilotic tongues of the southern Sudan belong, suggests strongly that they represent the remnants of what was once a homogeneous group of related languages scattered over a wide area of eastern Africa and centred on the Sudan. It is a not unreasonable hypothesis that this is where Meroitic belongs and it would explain the points of resemblance to Nubian. There is also just a hint that Meroitic may be related to the little-known group of languages known as Koman, now spoken in a limited area up the Blue Nile and round Jebel Gule.[7] This group is not included in the eastern Sudanic family, but it does belong to the wider grouping of Chari-Nile tongues which takes in the latter. A recent article by Trigger[8] makes a firmer claim for the inclusion of Meroitic in the eastern Sudanic grouping and produces a number of interesting parallels between Meroitic and various languages of the larger category.[9]

Meroitic has, with Etruscan, the distinction of being one of the two ancient languages the phonetic values of whose signs can be read with reasonable certainty, but the meaning of whose words cannot be understood. Its inscriptions are of two kinds; those in hieroglyphs, based on Egyptian prototypes, and those in the distinctive Meroitic writing, usually known inaccurately as 'cursive'. The letters in this form of writing are not joined, and therefore it is not, strictly speaking, legitimate to call it cur, sive; but the term is now so widely used that it is best to retain it here.

During Napatan times the official language of the country was Egyptian, though Meroitic may have been the colloquial speech. All the inscriptions of the period are in Egyptian, but the knowledge of that language became less and less, and, as time went on, these inscriptions showed increasing corruption and unfamiliarity with the rules of Egyptian grammar and orthography. The earliest Meroitic inscription to which any date can be given is that of Queen Shanakdakhete (*c.* 180–170 BC), found in a temple at Naqa. The earlier Meroitic inscriptions are in hieroglyphs, but cursive replaces them increasingly and after the time of Netekamani there are few hieroglyphic in, scriptions. The latest seems to be the name of King Tarcke, niwal inscribed on the pylon of his pyramid, Beg. N. 19, and dated to some time in the early second century AD.

The first attempts at decipherment by Griffith are to be found in his chapter on the inscriptions from Areika.[10] Here he estab, lished that the hieroglyphs, unlike Egyptian ones, were purely alphabetic, as their paucity suggested; and that, contrary to the Egyptian practice, the direction in which the hieroglyphs of men, animals and birds faced was the one to be adopted by the reader.

The vital inscription, which made possible the discovery of the phonetic values, was on the base for a sacred boat found by Lepsius at Wad ben Naqa and first published by him.[11] Here two royal names Netekamani and Amanitare, were written in both Egyptian and Meroitic hieroglyphs. Since the Egyptian was well known, the names could be read and equivalent phonetic values could thus be given to the Meroitic hieroglyphs.

The inscriptions were:

1. Egyptian

giving the name Netekamani with the usual honorific inver‚
sion, by which the name of the god (Amun) was given first
though read last,

    Meroitic

2. Egyptian

               Amanitare

    Meroitic

From these names, certain correlations were possible, and it
could be seen that the Meroitic hieroglyphic system was based
on a selection and modification of the Egyptian system. So the
first eight signs were identified and are given in the table below
with the Egyptian signs from which they were derived:

= n : Egyptian ⁓ = n

= m : Egyptian = m

= g or k : acrophonic from Egyptian = gb or $k\underline{t}$

= t : Egyptian = $\underline{t}$

= i : Egyptian = i ; HI in Old Coptic

= t : uncertain, possibly Egyptian = ta

= r or l : Egyptian = r

= y : Egyptian = y

This gave the sounds of eight out of a total of twenty three signs used. By this time, the equivalence of the hieroglyphic and cursive alphabets had been found from a comparison of funerary formulae. It was observed that these formulae, on offering tables and stelae, usually began with

$$\text{4-)IIS ω)3∶4-3/8}$$

and one offering table from Meroe was inscribed in hieroglyphs and began

$$\text{𓂝44β=𐤠 𓏤𓏤𓏤 ∶ 𓂝 𓏤𓏤𓏤 𐤠 𓎛}$$

The equivalence was clear and immediately gave the value for seven cursive signs:

$$8 = 𓎛 \qquad 5 = β \qquad /// = 44$$
$$3 = 𓏤𓏤𓏤 \qquad 4 = 𓂝 \qquad / = 𐤠$$
$$ω = ▱$$

These equivalents were confirmed and extended by further groups in the same text and a few others, until twenty-one cursive signs were identified with their hieroglyphic counter-parts. So, at this stage, phonetic values were established for eight signs in both alphabets. Then by a brilliant analysis Grif-fith distinguished the vowel signs in the cursive alphabet and so equally for the hieroglyphs.[12] The cursive signs so distin-guished are

$$/, 5, 4, 52.$$

Further values were then discovered by reference to place and other names until the phonetic values of signs had been estab-lished with a reasonable degree of certainty, enabling the follow-ing table to be given:

Hieroglyph	Cursive	Value	Hieroglyph	Cursive	Value
		initial aleph or *a*			l
		e			ḫ (kh)
		ê			ḫ (kh)
		i			s
		y			š (sh)
		w			k
		b			q
		p			t
		m			te
		n			tê
		ñ			d
		r			stop to separate words

That this interpretation cannot be far wrong is shown by the close resemblance of the Meroitic hieroglyphic forms to well-known Egyptian ones, and even some of the cursive signs are very similar to Egyptian demotic.[13] The rest of the cursive signs show no obvious derivation from Egyptian and we cannot say whence the inspiration for them came – they may have been a spontaneous local invention. Though it is likely that, in the main, the phonetic equivalents are right, there remains some doubt about the values of the vowel signs, and the several writings for '*t*' or '*t* and a vowel' are somewhat suspicious. In addition to the identification of the phonetic values, it was also seen that two or three vertical dots were used as word-dividers.

Griffith was able to make some progress in understanding the very large number of funerary inscriptions on the offering tables found in cemeteries, notably at Shablul and Karanog[14] and this has been carried a stage further by Hintze.[15] More than two hundred examples of this class of inscription are now known, some on offering tables and some on stelae. They show a common pattern, and all but very few begin with the words *weši: šereyi.* Normally, after this there is a different group in all the texts, followed by a double phrase, the halves of which begin with *ate* and *at.* Assuming that the name of the deceased is given, the only place for it is in the third group; it is here that the texts give us very great variations, and in many cases there is a series of words which can be presumed to give titles, ancestry and so on.

So the scheme of these funerary monuments seems to be that they begin with an invocation and, from Egyptian demotic inscriptions of similar type at Philae, it is virtually certain that the first two words are Isis and Osiris, 'O Isis, O Osiris'; they then continue with the name, parentage, and description of the person, and finish with a formula which is presumably a prayer.

The second part of the formula is sometimes a single word, varying from text to text, and thus likely to be a name. But this section, coming before the *ate* formula, is sometimes extensive, and in nearly all cases where there are several words we find amongst them *terikelewi* and *tdhelewi* with slight variations. The pattern in the shorter versions of the texts is A (name of deceased), B *tdhelewi*, C *terikelewi*. The B and C words vary from text to text and can therefore, like A, be taken as names, and the whole section can be assumed to mean A, son of B and C.

Identification of the sex of B and C is guessed from the common occurrence of the letter *r* at the end of the C name but not with B. Since, from known names, *r* seems to be a male termination, B will be the mother and C the father. So the whole formula can now be read as A, born of B, begotten of C or something very similar. A curious feature of these texts is the repetition, in many cases, of the words *terikelewi* and *tdhelewi,* frequently twice, in a few instances three times, and once[16] four times. In these cases of repetition, the ending *-ewi* is found only with the last reiteration of the words, which in other positions end with *-l*. The meaning of this repetition is far from clear. Griffith saw that the reiterations were genealogically equivalent to the single expression and went on to say, 'One can only conclude that the reduplication is intended to emphasize the reality of the parentage.' Hintze has suggested that it refers to the number of times the parent had been married; thus, in a theoretical example such as A, B, *tdhel tdhelewi,* C *terikelewi,* the deceased A would be born of the second marriage of the mother and the first of the father.[17]

Apart from this only partially successful attempt to interpret the funerary inscriptions, a few words have been made out, most of them loan words such as *tewisti* – adoration, *pelames* – a general or commander, *perite* – an agent, all borrowings from Egyptian. A few Meroitic words, whose suggested meanings have an element of guesswork in them are: *ate* – water, *wayeki* – star, *demi* – year, *mash* – sun, *kdi* – woman. All of these have Nubian cognates and it is this which has made possible their interpretation.

Attempts have been made to analyse grammatical elements, but they are all highly speculative. Certain points emerge; there seems to be no grammatical gender, the mark of the plural seems to be *eb* or *-b,* and postpositions, as in Nubian, seem to be widely used. That is as far as our knowledge goes at present, and it seems improbable that any further advance can be made on internal evidence alone. Failing the finding of a bilingual text, of which the most likely would be one in Egyptian and Meroitic, the most promising line of approach is the study of living languages which are in the right geographical area to suggest a relationship, however distant, to Meroitic. Meroitic itself has certainly become extinct, but from our knowledge of the history of African languages, it seems improbable that there are not still in use some which are related. Ancient Egyptian is also now extinct, except for the liturgical use of Coptic, but many related languages still continue to be widely spoken in Africa.[18]

The linguistic history of the area presents a number of problems, amongst which the origin of Nubian is relevant. Nubian is known to have been the language of the medieval Christian states of the Sudan, but the date of its introduction into the Nile Valley remains obscure. The first evidence we have for it is in writings of the tenth century AD but it must certainly have been in use before that time; it is not an unreasonable hypothesis that it was introduced by the Noba, and replaced Meroitic as the main language at some time after the beginning of the fourth century.

We know nothing of the spoken language of pre-Meroitic times, and it is possible that Nubian not Meroitic, was the tongue of the riverain population from the Pharaonic period. The present distribution of the various dialects of Nubian can be interpreted as being due to the disruption of a widespread Nubian linguistic area by Arabic from the fourteenth century onwards just as easily as it can by the more usual view that it was a language of the west, brought to the river by invading Noba. If this hypothesis has any value then it is necessary to see in Meroitic a ruling-class language; that such a situation is feasible can be seen from examples in Africa today, where in some parts chiefly families speak one language, and those they rule another.

CHAPTER VI

Religion and Burial Customs

U NTIL WE CAN READ the language, the sources for an appreciation of Meroitic religion are restricted to the temple reliefs and what little the classical writers tell us. The information given by these writers is not very helpful, since they showed little understanding of how the beliefs of others could differ from those they themselves held, and frequently attempt, as they did in describing Egyptian religion, to identify local gods with their own.

A study of the many deities depicted in the monuments reveals that the Meroitic people derived most of their official religious ideas from Egypt, and the majority of their gods and their iconography always remained closely similar to those of the Pharaohs. But they did have gods of their own which had no Egyptian counterparts, and one at least of these, Apedemek, became the most important god of the Island of Meroe. We have no knowledge of the indigenous religion of Kush during the period of Egyptian occupation, but Napatan religious practice seems to have been an exact copy of the Theban religion of the later New Kingdom with the dominance of Amun, who was as much the state god of Napata as he was of Egypt. The temple of Jebel Barkal was consecrated to the worship of Amun and, as we have seen, it remained an important religious centre long after the political power of Napata had waned.

The earlier Meroitic kings certainly regarded allegiance to Amun as a main element in their tenure of the throne and we know from the inscriptions of Amani-nete-yerike, Harsiotef, and Nastasen of the veneration in which he was held. The inscriptions are not only in the Egyptian language, but, in the religious ideas which they reveal, show complete conformity with Egyptian thought. It may be that this official religion, derived as it was from the religious observances of the earlier Egyptian occupation, was restricted to the royal family, their court, and the temple priesthoods.

The temple and pyramid chapel reliefs give us many representations of gods, and here again through the whole period of Meroitic history the gods are mainly Egyptian. In the reliefs of the pyramid chapels at Meroe, although they depart on occasion from Egyptian artistic ideas, the gods shown are only those known and represented in contemporary Egypt.

To find examples of independent Meroitic divinities we have to go to the temples, and here the reliefs from the Lion Temple at Musawwarat esSofra are of special importance. The temple is dedicated to the Liongod Apedemek,[1] unknown in the Egyptian pantheon, who was a divinity of great importance to the Meroites, but apparently not known in the northern part of the kingdom. The reliefs and inscriptions on this temple give us much information about Meroitic religion in the third century BC and are worth some detailed attention. Taking the south wall first, we see the king facing left with the goddess Isis behind him; in front of him is a smaller figure, a prince, described as priest of Isis of '*Iprbr'nh* and *Irbyklb,* two place names which occur frequently in these texts and have been tentatively identified as being of Musawwarat esSofra and Wad ben Naqa respectively.[2] In front of the king stands a line of six gods headed by Apedemek; he holds a bow and arrows in his left hand and also a cord to which a prisoner is tied. His whole appearance as well as his equipment suggests strongly that we have here a warrior god of extreme importance. The frequent references to him in Meroitic texts make clear his role and it seems that, together with Amun, he was the main god of the Meroites. The lion was his emblem, and this animal which must have roamed the Island of Meroe in considerable numbers, was certainly captured, probably when young, and kept at Musawwarat where it played some part in the ceremonies of the temple. One of the reliefs from this temple shows a lion cub being carried in procession, and another shows a tame seated lion with collar and leash. Following Apedemek is Amun, here taking second place, as the temple is dedicated to the Lion-god, but still a figure of power and significance. He is followed by another god in human and Egyptianised form but bearing a name not otherwise known, Sebewyemeker; then come Arensnuphis, Horus, and Thoth. Arensnuphis seems to be restricted to Nubia and is familiar from Philae; thus he may be in origin a Meroitic god. The last two are well-known Egyptian deities. On the north wall is a similar scene with the king and prince again facing a line of gods. Parts of this wall have been damaged and it is not possible to be certain of the identities of all the divine figures, but the leading one is again Apedemek, followed by an unidentified goddess, a god and another goddess, then by Amun shown this time – as commonly – with a ram's head, and behind him the goddess Satis, Horus, and Isis.

The particular importance of these reliefs is that they are inscribed in Egyptian with prayers to the gods or utterances by them, and therefore disclose something of the worshippers' attitude towards their deities. The prayer to Apedemek runs:

Thou art greeted, Apedemek, lord of Naqa;[3] great god, lord of Musawwarat es-Sofra; splendid god, at the head of Nubia. Lion of the south, strong of arm. Great god, the one who comes to those who call him. The one who carries (?) the secret, concealed in his being, who was not seen by any eye. Who is a companion for men and women, who will not be hindered in heaven and earth. Who procures nourishment for all men, in this his name 'Perfect Awakener'. The one who hurls his hot breath against his enemy, in this his name 'Great of Power'. Who kills the enemy with —. The one who punishes all who commit crimes against him. Who prepares the place for those who give themselves to him. Who gives to those who call to him. Lord of life, great in his sight.[4]

This prayer has many analogies with Egyptian religious texts of the Ptolemaic period and shows that, though Apedemek himself was a purely Meroitic god, those who composed the prayers to him were well aware of Egyptian ritual procedure.

The first part of the inscription of Sebewyemeker, however, has no Egyptian parallels and, as the god himself is known only from here, it is of particular interest in showing a purely local religious development. The god says:

'I give you everything which comes forth by night, everything which happens by day. I give to you the years of the sun, and the months of the moon in joy. So speaks Sebewyemeker lord of Musawwarat es Sofra, who gives life like the sun god for ever.'

And in another place,

'I give you the life time of the sun god in heaven, so speaks Sebewyemeker, the great god at the head of Nubia.'

We know no more of this god than these inscriptions tell us, but his association with Apedemek on the back wall of the Lion Temple, where they are the only two gods shown, suggests that he was one of the chief gods of the place, though not known as yet from any other Meroitic site. From what the god himself says, he appears to be a creator god, and it is perhaps significant that on this wall of the temple a frieze of ankh signs, the sign of life, lies beneath his feet, whilst beneath the feet of Apedemek, the war god, are to be seen bound prisoners tied to war elephants.

Sebewyemeker is known only from Musawwarat es-Sofra but his greater associate the Lion-god is known from a number of other places of which Naqa, where also a temple is dedicated to him, is the most important. In this remarkable and unique representation at Naqa (see p. 89), on the exterior of the back wall, Apedemek stands as the sole god receiving adoration from the royal family. He is shown only on the southern of the two exteriors of the two side walls, where, as at Musawwarat es-Sofra, he heads a line of gods approached and adored by the king, queen, and prince. Here he is followed by Horus, Amun, Khonsu, and Khnum. The opposite wall also shows the royal family but this time in front of a series of goddesses, Isis, Mut, an unknown goddess of African appearance, perhaps the sole representation of an indigenous goddess, Hathor, and Satis. So here again is a portrayal of Egyptian deities with the addition of the Lion-god and the unknown goddess. All these divine figures are accompanied by short inscriptions in Meroitic hiero-glyphs[5] which in some cases give their names, but are not other-wise intelligible.

On two pylons of this temple a lion is represented as aiding the king and queen to defeat their enemies; on the outer sides of the pylons Apedemek is shown with the body of a snake emerging from a flower. His standard is depicted on the back wall transfixing an enemy. Thus all parts of the temple bear testimony to the power of the Lion-god who is also represented at other places throughout the Island of Meroe, in the Lion Temple, at the town of Meroe, and at Basa; while Umm Usuda, 'The mother of lions' (see p. 96), seems to enshrine in its name this powerful god.

It has been suggested[6] that Apedemek is also to be regarded as a manifestation of the sun, and that the cult of the lion and that of the sun are identical. The evidence for this is not ap-parent in representations of Apedemek himself, the idea being based on analogies with the sun cult in Syria and Persia. Cer-tainly the plan of many of the small Meroitic temples – not only the peripteral type represented by the Sun Temple at Meroe and the temple in the central complex at Musawwarat es-Sofra, but also the small chamber, or *cella*, containing four columns – is closely paralleled in Western Asia, and this may be evidence of influence from that area.[7] If this view is correct, the Sun-god incised in the rock at Jebel Qeili, which has a strong hint of Hellenistic Syrian style, may be the same god in another guise.

Fig. 33

Fig. 34

He is certainly shown as a god of military victory, in the same way as is Apedemek.

Another local cult was that of the elephant, which is frequently depicted at Musawwarat es-Sofra. No representation that we can interpret as an elephant god is to be seen there, though architectural details featuring elephants make it clear that parts of the complex were devoted to practices having this animal as their theme. From Wad ben Naqa there is, however, a small statue[8] ostensibly of a divinity in the form of an elephant, and there can be little doubt that both elephant and lion were regarded as divine.

Some confirmation of Herodotus' view concerning the cult of Isis and Osiris for funerary purposes can be seen in the very large number of funerary offering tables with invocations to these gods (p. 138). Since Osiris was the traditional Egyptian god of the dead and Isis his wife, here once more Egyptian ideas can be seen to dominate. Many of these offering tables show the goddess Nephthys and the god Anubis, both concerned with the cult of the dead in Egypt, pouring libations. Although the form of these offering tables and the inscriptions are Meroitic, the theological ideas embodied are Egyptian.

The existence of another Sun-god has been assumed from the occurrence of the name *Mesh* in many funerary texts in the large northern cemeteries at Karanog and Shablul.[9] Since our understanding of these texts is so slight, this is still a matter for conjecture, but it is an interesting suggestion; there may have been a local cult with perhaps a temple as yet undiscovered.[10]

BURIAL CUSTOMS

Meroitic burial customs show the same mixture of local and Egyptian traditions as are to be seen in all other aspects of the culture. The very earliest royal burials at Kurru, dating from before the rise of Meroe, show the continuation of a tradition

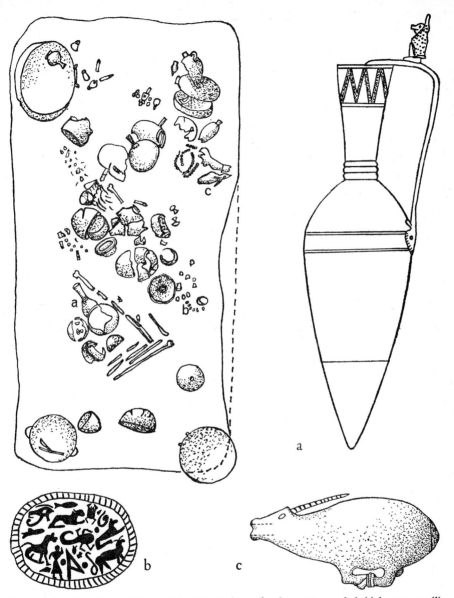

Fig. 51. Burial W. 609 at Meroe, and three individual items found at positions marked: (a) bronze vase; (b) glazed steatite scarab; (c) alabaster vase

where the body was buried on a bed as in the much earlier cemetery of about 1800 BC at Kerma.[11] This custom was modi-fied to the extent that the bodies were mummified in the Egyp-tian manner, and canopic jars, in which some of the internal organs were preserved as well a full range of Egyptian amulets and *shawabtis*,[12] were found. By the time the Nuri cemetery was being used the custom had almost died out and only a few of the earliest burials were on beds. Instead, the normal Egyptian practice of burial in a stone or wooden coffin became the in-variable rule, making them indistinguishable from Egyptian burials. Some of them must have been extremely rich, for even the much-plundered tombs yielded a great deal of material, and amulets and *shawabtis* were found in profusion.

The cemeteries at Meroe add considerably to our knowledge of the burial rites. The earliest graves of the South and West Cemeteries, those in use before the time of Aspelta, are of especial interest since here the two traditions can be seen existing contemporaneously. Two quite different types of burial were found. The first, or native type, consisted of a rectangular grave in which the non-mummified body was laid, usually on its left side, on a wooden bed as in the early burials at Kurru. These burials contained rich grave goods of a type known from the Kurru and earlier Nuri cemeteries. Tomb W. 609[13] in the West Cemetery is a good example of this class of burial; it con-tained a large number of faience amulets, as well as beads, ala-baster bowls and vessels of silver and bronze. The content of the other burials is much poorer; they are narrower and contain mummified bodies placed in wooden coffins and frequently covered with a bead net of a type well known from contempo-rary burials in Egypt. Tomb W. 671, though comparatively rich in its grave goods for burials of this class, is in other respects representative. The presence of contemporary burials of two such distinctive kinds is remarkable and it has been suggested that there were two separate communities living at Meroe at

Fig. 51

Fig. 52

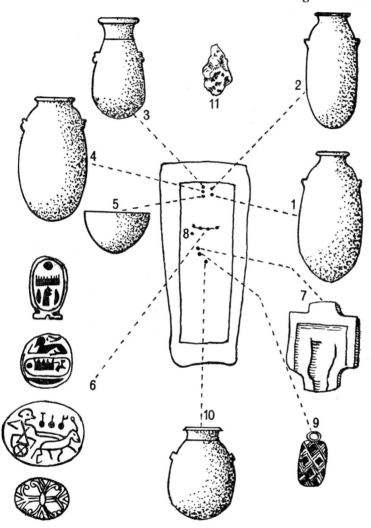

Fig. 52. Burial W. 671 at Meroe, showing positions of items found: 1–5, 10, alabaster jars; 6, four of the ten scarabs or scaraboid seals; 7, amulet of amazon stone, in the shape of an offering bath; 8, the remains of a bead net; 9, cylindrical stone pebble encased in an open gold-work cover; 11, a gold nugget found lying loose

149

this time; that the bed burials are those of the local Meroitic aristocracy, whilst the coffin burials of Egyptian type are those of a colony of Egyptian artisans and scribes.

As at Nuri, the bed burials do not seem to continue into full Meroitic times, and coffin burials become the standard practice for the rest of the period; so many of the burials were plundered and damaged, however, that very little evidence remains, particularly from the royal burials in the north cemetery where in only rare instances coffins or their traces have been found. Two pyramid tombs, N. 11 and N. 12, contained stone coffins; in many others stood stone benches on which, it is reasonable to suppose, coffins once lay. Presumably many of these coffins were of wood, but identifiable remains have been found only in pyramids N. 15 and N. 17, both from the second century AD. It can be inferred that mummification continued well into Meroitic times, but the bodies have all been so damaged by robbers that we cannot be certain how long the custom continued.

From the early first century AD we find multiple burials. In most cases these consist of a principal burial in a coffin with a number of uncoffined skeletons lying on the floor of the grave; this looks like reversion to the custom of sacrificial burials such as those at Kerma, where servants were slaughtered to accompany their master after death. In some instances the skeletons of animals have also been found in the graves.

The cemetery of mound graves which lies to the east of the pyramids was mainly post-Meroitic and bed burials were again found. Cemetery 500 is of Meroitic date but no information is available as to the nature of the burials, though such description as there is makes it clear that these are the tombs of much poorer people than those of the great royal cemeteries. The grave goods seem to have consisted mainly of pottery, with a few beads and an occasional offering table.

The large cemeteries of the north[15] provide the best information on the burial customs of commoners. Karanog and Faras

Fig. 53. Funerary stelae from Karanog (after Woolley and MacIver)

were the two largest and although there are small local variations, there is sufficient consistency to generalize about the customs in use. The bodies were not mummified and the majority
were[16] buried without coffins and laid at full length on their
backs, generally wrapped in cloth. At Karanog this cloth was
said to be linen, whereas at Meroe cotton has been found. Grave
goods were placed in the tombs in some quantity, consisting
usually of pottery, though bronze vessels, beads and rings and
other trinkets were not uncommon. In a number of instances
men had their bows and arrows buried with them, and a few
spearheads have also been found, but apparently no other
weapons were placed in the graves.

In front of the entrance to the tomb it was normal to place an
offering table,[17] usually but not invariably, inscribed. Occasionally there were stelae, and the curious half-human, half-bird
figures which in Egyptian religion represented the soul. Most of
them when found had been overturned and it was seldom possible to be certain to which grave they belonged, or where they
originally stood, although it seems probable that they were
placed above ground and in a niche in the superstructure of
the tombs.

Figs. 35, 36
Fig. 53
Plate 37

This necessarily brief survey gives some account of the funerary customs so far observed but it is based only on the partial
evidence of royal burials in the south and commoners' burials
in the north. Until a number of non-royal burials have been
examined in the southern province we shall not have a full
picture of Meroitic practice, nor can we yet determine whether
the different grave types in the northern cemeteries denote different social groups. However, the variation in the richness of
grave goods as noted at Faras (see p. 65) suggests that this may
be the case.

CHAPTER VII

The People and their Life: Meroe and Africa

Since we cannot read the Meroitic language and since we have no such wealth of information about daily life as the tomb paintings of Ancient Egypt provide, the life and society of the time can be reconstructed only by study of the archaeological material, and so few dwelling sites have so far been excavated that this remains scanty. The discovery of palaces, temples, and cemeteries provides important artistic and historical information, but tells little of the life of the people, of their homes, their agriculture, or their social organization; we can only guess at this from the scattered remains that have come to us from the past.

If we do not know how the Meroitic state was organized, nor how its kings and queens maintained their rule, we do know that it was a monarchical state, and we can assume that, as in Egypt, the king was regarded as divine; but of lesser rulers, courtiers, and chiefs, we know nothing. Queens played an important part in the life of the country, and ruled at times in their own right. If, as seems likely, the society was a matrilineal one, they would have been the transmitters of royal property as well as of succession to the throne. Without written documents it is difficult to be sure of this, but there is some evidence from Napatan times that the royal family, for its part, was matrilineal;[1] we know too that in the Christian state of Nubia which succeeded Meroe the same system prevailed, and that queen mothers were held in special veneration.[2] The prominence given to queens in Meroitic temple and chapel reliefs strongly suggests that the same system prevailed at Meroe.

At the part played in society by priests and military leaders we can only guess. From hints in the classical writers we know that priests were a powerful influence; places like Musawwarat es-Sofra and Naqa were probably largely inhabited by those dedicated to the temple service, and it seems possible that, as in Egypt, the priesthood owned considerable property. The Sun Temple reliefs with their scenes of military victory hint at war-like organization and leadership; but even if we could fully interpret them, they would be unlikely to tell us much about how the armies of Meroe were raised, organized, or led; still less about social conditions lower down the scale.

PHYSICAL APPEARANCE

The physical appearance of the people has been the subject of considerable discussion, but until we have detailed studies of a large sample of skeletal material, it will not be possible to speak with any certainty. The many representations of royal persons do not greatly help, though African features may be inferred in some cases. The old notion that the ancestors of the Kushite royal family were Libyans has now been largely abandoned in favour of the view that they were of local Napatan origin, but we know too little of the indigenous population of Kush at the time for this to tell us very much of the ethnic composition of the royal family. Taharqa is shown as a Negro on the stela of the Assyrian King Esarhaddon at Sinjirli;[3] this is, however, not in itself decisive. The representation is probably not a portrait, but more likely merely the Assyrian artist's conventional representation for a man from the far south. The excavators of Kara-nog[4] claimed that the majority of the skeletons found there were negroid, but these results were not based on expert study, and they should be treated with some reserve. Personal observation of bodies from Nubia, where in some cases the features have been well preserved, suggests that the physical type was much the same as in modern times. Few examinations of skeletal material from Meroe have been made, but three skulls found in the tomb of King Amanitenmemide (Beg. N.17) have been

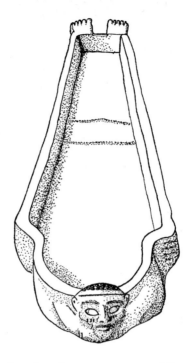

Fig. 54. Pottery coffin from Argin

studied; of these one was said to be of Mediterranean type whilst the other two were faintly negroid.[5] Nubia, together with most of the northern Sudan, is today inhabited by a predominantly brown-skinned people of aquiline features having in varying degrees an admixture of Negro, and there is no reason to suppose that the ancient populations were very different.

Persistence of cultural traits from the ancient population is seen in the face cuts, still in use as decoration and as tribal marks in the Sudan, though they are now becoming rare. Such scarification was practised in Meroitic times, and a pot from Faras shows cuts on the cheek of the lion's victim, and similar ones are to be seen on a very unusual human-headed coffin from Argin.[6] Blue facial tattoo marks characterize some of the bodies from Meroitic cemeteries in Nubia, and this may have been a common practice. Antimony was used by women as eye paint,

Plate 46

Fig. 54

155

Fig. 58

as is still customary in many parts of Africa and the Near East, and the special pots for containing the powdered antimony[7] and the sticks with which it was applied have been found in some numbers. Other cosmetics were certainly used and the numerous finds of glass vessels imported as containers for oils and un-guents as well as the mirrors show that Meroitic ladies, at least of the richer classes, took considerable trouble over their ap-pearance.

DOMESTIC BUILDINGS

Fig. 3

We know little of the domestic buildings of the Meroites and few ordinary houses have been discovered. The buildings of the royal city at Meroe cannot be taken as typical and the majority of people will have lived, then as now, in simple huts of sun-dried brick or of straw. The bronze bowl from Karanog, the only illustration we have of domestic life of the time, shows us a straw hut which may be regarded as typical. Circular in shape, it is very similar to many huts to be seen in Africa today, and it is topped by an object which is probably an ostrich egg – a good luck, or fertility symbol, still to be seen on many houses and huts in East and West Africa.

Fig. 55

There are few examples of brick-built houses. On the op-posite page is shown the plan of one such on the island of Gaminarti in the Second Cataract; it can be seen to be of some size and complexity, and was solidly built of sun-dried brick, with walls that stood to a height of well over six feet. One of the features of this house, repeated in others, is its arrangement in groups of two rooms, of which the smaller one is entered from the larger. The cooking pots and the fireplace have always been found in the main room, which must also have been used for living and sleeping in, so far as these activities took place indoors; the smaller room seems to have been a store.[8] The few other houses of the period of which we know conform to this

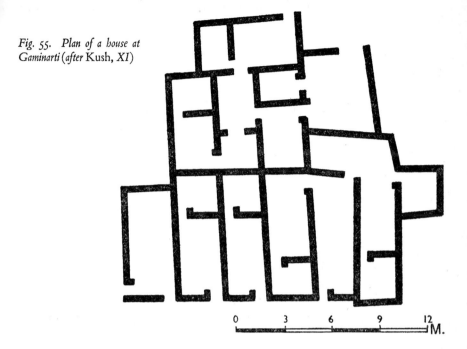

Fig. 55. Plan of a house at Gaminarti (after Kush, XI)

0   3   6   9   12 M.

pattern and were presumably the dwelling places of a small community, or large extended family, each set of two rooms forming a unit within the whole building.

FURNITURE

Little remains of the furnishing of these houses, though from the presence of beds in tombs we can assume that they were also used by the living. These beds are of a type still used and known in Arabic as *angareeb,* consisting of a wooden frame with an interlacing of rope or leather thongs to form a mattress. This style of bed is of considerable antiquity in the Nile Valley the earliest known example being one found at Kerma[9] and dating from the first half of the second millennium BC. Of other furniture there is little trace, but we know from reliefs that kings at least sat on chairs. A folding stool with bronze and silver

Fig. 56

157

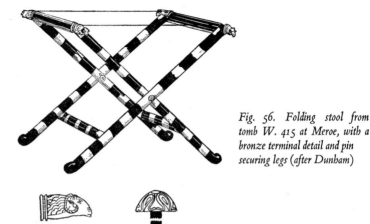

Fig. 56. Folding stool from tomb W. 415 at Meroe, with a bronze terminal detail and pin securing legs (after Dunham)

fittings was found in one grave at Meroe[10] and fragments of others are known.

Here perhaps mention can be made of a number of small wooden and ivory boxes which have been found in the graves. It is not certain that any of these were produced by Meroitic craftsmen; a wooden one made to contain a number of glass vessels probably came in from Egypt with the glass it contained,[11] and the very well-preserved ones from Karanog with ivory insets[12] are certainly imported. Others such as the little box from Beg. N. 30[13] with its carefully made dovetailed corners, and the oval one from Bar. 2,[14] may have been made locally.

AGRICULTURE

The main activity of most of the Meroitic people will have been in various forms of agriculture, and we know that cattle-rearing and the growing of grain crops played an important part in their life. The Karanog bronze bowl mentioned above is evidence for the herding of cattle, and they are also shown in considerable numbers in chapel reliefs. On the bowl the tend⁄ ing and milking of cattle is shown, and a female figure, in many ways similar to the queens of the temple reliefs, is shown seated in front of a hut accompanied by two other females and receiv⁄ ing milk which is about to be poured from a large wooden(?) vessel into a number of bowls placed on the ground in front of her. Behind the man who is pouring are the cattle, and one cow, which is being milked, wears a bell. Such bells have been found (p. 129) and from the scene on the bowl we can assume that they were affixed, as today, to one animal in each herd. For other domestic animals we have less evidence, and we know little about the keeping of sheep and goats, though they were certainly present. The horse was used for both riding and pull⁄ ing chariots and on occasion horses were buried with their masters[15], but we do not find the degree of devotion to this animal shown in earlier times by Piankhy nor later by the X⁄ Group rulers, who frequently had their steeds buried with them. The elephant, perhaps used only for ritual purposes, has already been discussed (p. 101), whilst the camel, so important in the area today, was not common along the Nile until the beginning of the Christian era and only one Meroitic representation of it is known.

Of food crops we know only what the classical writers tell us. Strabo, for example, specifically mentions millet,[16] presum⁄ ably the *sorghum vulgare,* which under the name of *dhurra* is the main crop of the modern Sudan. It seems to be represented in the scene at Jebel Qeili (p. 96). The discovery of fragments of cloth made of cotton suggests that this plant was also grown, and the presence of spindle whorls and loom weights shows that it was locally spun and woven. The introduction of cotton may be another example of Indian influence on Meroitic civi⁄ lization.[17] Small fragments of cloth made from flax show that it too was used, but it is more likely that such cloth was made in Egypt and imported than that it was locally grown. It is

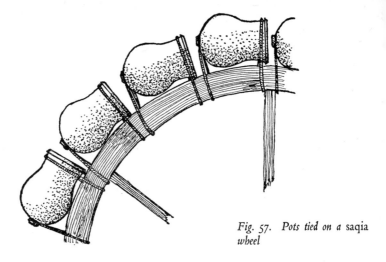

Fig. 57. *Pots tied on a* saqia *wheel*

certainly more common in the northern cemeteries than in those of the capital.

On the Island of Meroe rain irrigation could be used for all these crops. Where they were grown further north, water must have been raised from the river either by *shaduf*, the simple apparatus consisting of a long pole with a water container at one end counterbalanced by a lump of clay at the other, which is of great antiquity along the Nile; or by means of the *saqia*, the ox-driven water-wheel whose introduction made such a difference to the Meroitic occupation of lower Nubia. The special pots used to lift the water, easily identified by the knob on the base by which they were tied to the wheel, are found in quantity on riverside sites.

Fig. 57

IRON-WORKING

The many large mounds of iron slag are probably the remains by which the town of Meroe is now best known. They have been the cause of much speculation on the importance of iron in the Meroitic economy, and their presence at this site is largely responsible for the view that the knowledge of iron-working in Africa spread from Meroe. The six large mounds of slag within the boundaries of the town certainly indicate areas where iron was smelted, but none of them has yet been examined in detail and no study of the techniques involved has been made. It is likely that the methods used were similar to those widely current in Africa until recently, where the ore was smelted in simple furnaces fired by charcoal,[18] the material for which was abundantly at hand in the groves of acacia trees growing in profusion along the Nile. The raw material for the iron itself was also easily available in the ironstone formation which caps the sandstone hills over much of the northern Sudan and in quantity in the Island of Meroe. The fortunate occurrence of the two basic requirements for iron production – the ore and the fuel – in one place was of great advantage to Meroe, and it was certainly due to the production of this metal that Meroitic power was maintained so long and that such great wealth was built up. Once iron was produced in sufficient quantity Meroitic troops would have had as marked an advantage over local adversaries, armed only with stone or sometimes copper weapons, as did the Assyrians when they first broke into Egypt in the seventh century BC. Though iron was introduced into the Nile Valley in some quantity by the Assyrians, it was neither quickly nor readily adopted by the Egyptians, and further south knowledge of the metal penetrated only slowly. Even in the middle of the fifth century BC, in speaking of the Ethiopian soldiers of the army of Xerxes, Herodotus reported that they did not have iron for arrowheads.

It seems probable that it was the Greek and Carian mercenaries of Psammetichus II who first brought iron weapons as far as Napata,[19] but very little use was made of this new material and only few and fragmentary pieces of iron have been found earlier than the time of Harsiotef in the early part of the fourth century BC.[20] Iron models of tools were found in the foundation deposits of the king's pyramid and from that time on the metal was increasingly used.

The earliest pieces were certainly imports, and we do not know when the technique of iron-smelting was learnt, but by the middle of the first century BC it is probable that the process was being used at Meroe as well as at other places.[21] From the beginning of the Christian era the metal becomes much more common, but it is likely that stone and bronze (or copper) continued to be used for tools and weapons, iron being found as the predominant material only in burials which are thought to be of very late or even post-Meroitic date. The X-group people made extensive use of iron and the area came into the full Iron Age only after the decline of Meroe.

TOOLS AND WEAPONS

The mastery of iron-working made a decisive difference to the nature as well as to the quantity of tools and weapons available to the Meroites; but since its introduction was slow and bronze continued in use over a long period, metal implements found in the earlier burials are all of this latter material. The source of Meroitic bronze is not known, and as there do not appear to be deposits of copper ore within easy reach, it is likely that many of the bronze objects were made in Egypt; it is also possible that ingots of metal were brought to Meroe where they could be worked locally.

Numerous bronze artifacts have been discovered, and in addition to such tools as adzes, hoe blades, axes, and chisels, many smaller articles like tweezers, and the little metal rods for applying antimony to the eyes are known. Larger iron tools are also found but are not common, though their rarity may be due partly to the rapid deterioration of iron, which corrodes very badly especially when affected by damp; hoe blades or mattocks, the main tool of the cultivators, have been found, as have adzes

Fig. 58. Metal rod for painting eyes with anti-mony

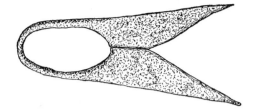

Fig. 59. Iron shears

which were extensively used in wood-working, axes, shears, and tweezers.

Fig. 59

Weapons are more plentiful than tools, since as objects of greater prestige, they were more commonly placed with the dead than were the workaday implements of agriculture and manu-facture. Swords and spears were used, but the main weapon of the Meroitic warriors seems to have been the bow and arrow, and arrowheads have been found in large numbers.

No swords have been found; they are known only from rep-resentations in sculptured reliefs, and even there they are com-paratively rare. The most interesting representation of a sword is at the Sun Temple at Meroe, where the scabbard is also shown, hanging on a strap from the shoulder, in the manner of the Beja of the Red Sea Hills at the present day. It has been suggested[22] that this weapon is the ancestor of swords now used by the Tuareg nomads of the central Sahara. On the Lion Temple at Naqa, King Netekamani is shown wielding a sword of rather different type. At Jebel Qeili, King Sherkarer appears in the full panoply of the Meroitic warrior; he has a sword in its scabbard worn over the shoulder as in the Sun Temple relief, a quiver, also over his shoulder, and in his left hand he carries a spear, a bow, and three arrows.

Axes were used as weapons, as well as for more mundane purposes, as is evidenced by representations of royal persons both at Meroe and at Naqa who can be seen to be holding them in their hands. The shape is distinctive and none of the fragmentary pieces found seem to be of this type, being more

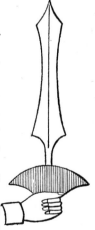

Fig. 60. Sword wielded by King Netekamani (after Budge)

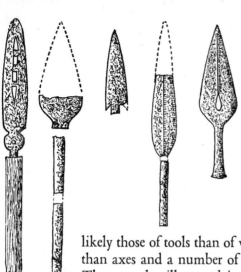

Fig. 61.   *Iron spearheads from Meroe (after Garstang)*

likely those of tools than of weapons. Spears are far commoner than axes and a number of iron spearheads have been found. They are also illustrated in many places in the reliefs, where they assume varying shapes.

Actual finds of bows are limited to doubtful fragments, since they are made of perishable materials, but their use is made clear by their common appearance in the hands of royal persons in the reliefs, as well as by the archer's draw rings of stone (p. 110) and arrowheads frequently found. In a few cases bundles of arrows have come to light still in the fragments of what were once quivers. The quivers were usually of leather and are

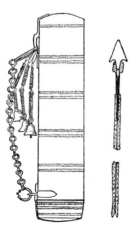

Fig. 62.   *Bronze quiver and arrow from tomb W. 122 at Meroe; the arrow has an iron head and ferrule, and a hardwood shaft set in a reed (after Dunham)*

normally found in a state of extreme decay, but one remarkable example in bronze containing seventy-three arrows, was found in the West Cemetery at Meroe.[23] The shafts of these arrows were of wood and cane, the heads of iron. Discolouration of the arrowheads and the careful way in which they had been placed in a metal quiver suggest that poisoned arrows were used. The great majority of arrowheads were of iron, but the discovery of a number made of carnelian confirms Herodotus' account of stone arrowheads. Of these, some were found at the town site of Meroe, a few in graves.

Fig. 62

The iron arrowheads vary considerably in shape; they are all tanged, but are both barbed and plain. One of the curious features is the number of harpoon-like heads with a single barb. It is not possible at present to say whether there is any chronological significance in the different shapes, but the single barbed ones seem to predominate in the later graves.

Fig. 63. Iron arrowhead

MEROE AND AFRICA

For long the least known and studied of all the ancient civilization of Africa and the Near East, Meroe now begins to take its place in the story of man's development and can be seen to have played a significant part in the history of north-east Africa. The renewal of active interest in the period stems largely from the development of historical studies in Africa, as well as from the view of many writers that it was Meroe that gave to much of the African continent the arts of civilization and government, and in particular the knowledge of metal-working.

It has been argued that after the end of Meroitic power in the fourth century AD the royal family migrated westwards,[24] taking with it specialized skills and techniques as well as concepts of state organization which then spread through the continent. This is an interesting and attractive hypothesis, but at present lacks any factual evidence to support it. The arguments on which it is based are not archaeological ones, and no Meroitic material has yet been found to the west of the Nile.

The oral traditions of some of the peoples of Darfur in the western Sudan which are said to retain memories of this move-ment cannot be considered reliable in view of the immense period of time involved, and suggestions that the word Kush survives in the name of the Kajiddi, a people of Jebel Meidob, and others having the element *Kaj* in their name should be regarded with some reserve. The finding of sherds of medieval Nubian pottery in the west,[25] as well as the spread of red-brick buildings from the Nile to Bornu in northern Nigeria,[26] makes it more likely that any Nilotic influences in West Africa came in later times, and were the result of westward movements by the inhabitants of Christian Nubia under the pressure of Arab invasion from the twelfth century AD onwards. Persistent leg-ends of Nilotic origins amongst many peoples of the regions of Chad and northern Nigeria, if they have any basis in reality, are more likely to be memories of influences coming from Christian Nubia than from Meroe.

There are also in Africa to the west and south of the Nile Valley many resemblances to ancient Egyptian beliefs and prac-tices; these as well as objects having an ostensible affinity with Egyptian ones, are often assumed to have come from Meroe. Such 'Egyptian' traits[27] may have been assimilated much ear-lier since Ancient Egypt's contacts with Africa beyond its southern frontiers go far back into Old Kingdom times. There is, moreover, no evidence that they, if anything more than coin-cidences, passed from Egypt to Africa and not the other way round. Many points of contact between Ancient Egyptian and African art and court rituals have been proposed,[28] but it needs a firm devotion to the theory of diffusion from Egypt to see in these supposed likenesses traces of Pharaonic and Meroitic cul-ture. In spite of this, there do remain objects which are remark-ably Egyptian in appearance – head-rests, musical instruments

and ostrich-feather fans are amongst the best known – and it
may be that it was from Meroe that the fashion for such things
spread. It should be noted that, in the main, the objects of
Egyptian appearance are not such as were known to have been
common in Meroe, and it should be emphasized that not a
single object of certain Meroitic origin has been found away
from the Nile to the west. Until some concrete evidence is
found, such ideas cannot be substantiated.

We are on slightly firmer ground in seeing Meroe as the
centre of dispersion of metal-working techniques, but even here
there is no more than supposition. The existence of a long and
skilled tradition of bronze-working by the *cire perdue* method
amongst the Yoruba and the Bini of Nigeria is of considerable
significance, and the question of where the knowledge of this
technique came from needs to be asked. It is possible that it
was an independent invention, but the complexity of the technique makes this a less likely solution than that it came from
outside. If this is so, the Nile Valley is by far the most likely
source from which such a skill could have been learnt. Unfortunately, the chronology of the forest cultures of West Africa
is still largely unknown and it cannot at present be established
that bronze-casting was being carried out there before the fourteenth or fifteenth century AD, so that we are faced with a long
gap between the date of the end of Meroe and the beginnings
of metal-work at Ife and Benin.

Iron-working is spread more widely. The coming of iron to
sub-Saharan Africa was an event of very great importance for
the development of the continent and caused a dramatic change
in way of life and in social and political organization. Most of
Africa went directly from a predominantly stone-using economy[29] to one incorporating the use of iron, though the introduction of this metal must have been gradual, and stone tools
and weapons continued long in use beside their iron counter-
parts. Who it was that taught the technique of iron-smelting

in Africa has not yet been determined, and decisive evidence as to the source of this knowledge, the routes by which it came, and the date of its arrival in various parts of Africa, would be of extreme value for the understanding of a crucial period in the history of the continent.

Recent work has shown us something of early iron-using communities, particularly in Central Africa, where dates, derived from Carbon 14, ranging from the sixth to the fourteenth centuries AD have been established.[30] From a study of these dates it appears that iron-working was introduced into that area in the second half of the first millennium AD. For other parts of the continent we have no such firm dates but can assume that the knowledge of iron-working was diffused at about the same time, although it may have been rather later in the forest areas of the Guinea coast.

Meroe seems an obvious place from which the new technique could have spread. While conceivably the main centre, however, it may not have been the only one; parts of West Africa, for example, could have received knowledge of the new material from the coast of North Africa by way of the Sahara caravan routes.[31] For Central and East Africa there is no other obvious place from which the knowledge of the use of iron could have come and the dates are quite consistent with the theory that there was a slow penetration southwards from the Nile in the first few centuries AD.

The real importance of Meroe for the history of Africa is not confined to its putative role as a disseminator of techniques and ideas. Meroe may well have inspired the great changes which the development of iron technology brought about. The use of iron not only enabled agriculture to make great strides through the use of the iron hoe, with the concomitant increase in production and therefore of population, but also, by providing iron weapons, made it possible for centralized authority to develop. The states which grew up in the Middle Ages, notably in the western Sudan (where the earliest one of which we know, Ghana, was already in existence by the eighth century AD and may be somewhat older) may conceivably have derived their ideas of state organization from Meroe;[32] they certainly depended for their authority on the superiority which the new metal gave to their armies.

Further research may well show in detail how the development of Meroitic civilization influenced other parts of the continent, and the presence of an ancient state, the outline of whose chronology is known, is of great potential value for the study of neighbouring territories. The establishment of a chronology is one of the most difficult tasks facing those working on the history of Africa, and the existence of material of approximately known date reaching far up the Nile into the heart of the continent is an essential aid in this work.

Whatever the role of Meroe may have been in the spread of culture amongst its neighbours, its own history stands as a major landmark of ancient Africa. Although much was owed to outside influences – and this book has attempted to show something of these – Meroe was an African civilization, firmly based on African soil, and developed by an African population. That an urban, civilized, and literate state existed deep in the African continent and lasted nearly a thousand years in itself constitutes an achievement of outstanding importance.

Notes on the text

Abbreviations

Arkell (1961):	A. J. Arkell, *A History of the Sudan* (2nd Edition, London, 1961).
BIFAO:	*Bulletin de l'Institut Français d'Archéologie Orientale.*
Budge (1907):	E. A. Wallis Budge, *The Egyptian Sudan,* 2 vols. (London, 1907).
Budge (1912):	E. A. Wallis Budge, *Annals of the Nubian Kings* (London, 1912).
Crawford (1953):	O. G. S. Crawford, *Castles and Churches in the Middle Nile Region,* Sudan Antiquities Service Occasional Papers No. 2. (Khartoum, 1953).
Crowfoot(1911):	J. W. Crowfoot, *The Island of Meroe* (London, 1911).
Garstang (1911):	J. Garstang, *Meroe – The City of the Ethiopians* (Oxford, 1911).
Griffith (1911a):	F. Ll. Griffith, *Karanog – The Meroitic Inscriptions of Shablul and Karanog* (Philadelphia, 1911).
Griffith (1911b):	F. Ll. Griffith *Meroitic Inscriptions* Part I, bound with Crowfoot (1911) (London, 1911).
Griffith (1912)	F. Ll. Griffith, Meroitic Inscriptions, Part II (London, 1912).
Hintze (1959):	F. Hintze, *Studien zur Meroitischen Chronologie und zu den Opfertafeln aus den Pyramiden von Meroe* (Berlin, 1959).
Hintze (1962):	F. Hintze, *Die Inschriften des Löwentempels von Musawwarat es Sofra* (Berlin, 1962).
JEA:	*Journal of Egyptian Archaeology.*
Kirwan (1939):	L. P. Kirwan, *The Oxford Excavations at Firka* (London, 1939).
LAAA:	*Liverpool Annals of Archaeology and Anthropology.*
Lepsius:	C. R. Lepsius, *Denkmäler aus Aegypten und Aethiopien,* Plates, 12 volumes (Berlin, 1849–59). Text, 5 volumes (Leipzig, 1897–1913).

Macadam   M.F. Laming Macadam, *The Temples of Kawa; I,*
(1949)   *The Inscriptions* (London, 1949).
Macadam   M.F. Laming Macadam, *The Temples of Kawa; II,*
(1955):   *History and Archaeology of the Site* (London, 1955).
MacIver (1909):   D. Randall MacIver and C.L. Woolley, *Areika* (Oxford, 1909).
Monneret de   U. Monneret de Villard, *Storia della Nubia Cristiana*
Villard (1938):   (Rome, 1938).
Porter and   B. Porter and R.C.B. Moss, *Topographical Bibliography*
Moss (1951):   VII (Oxford, 1951).
PSBA: *Proceedings of the Society of Biblical Archaeology.*
RCK: Dunham, *Royal Cemeteries of Kush:* I, *el Kurru* (Cambridge, Mass. 1950); II, *Nuri* (Boston, Mass. 1955); III, *Decorated Chapels of the Meroitic Pyramids at Meroe and Barkal* (Boston, 1952); IV, *Royal Tombs at Meroe and Barkal* (Boston, 1957); V, *The West and South Cemeteries at Meroe* (Boston, 1963).
SNR: *Sudan Notes and Records.*
Woolley (1910):   C.L. Woolley and D. Randall MacIver, *Karanog: The Romano-Nubian Cemetery* (Philadelphia, 1910).

CHAPTER I

1 R.E.M. Wheeler, *Rome Beyond the Imperial Frontiers* (London, 1955), 142.
2 *SNR*, XXVIII (1947), 11–24.
3 Garstang (1911), 25–27.
4 The modern name for the 'Island of Meroe'.
5 Hintze (1959), 28.
6 The area twelve *Schoeni* long lying south of the First Cataract.
7 *Kush*, IX (1961), 284–286. Hintze has recently found a squeeze made by Lepsius and publishes it in *Kush*, XII (1964), 296–298.
8 The modern name of this country is Ethiopia, but to prevent confusion with the Ethiopia of the ancients which normally means the modern Sudan, the older name is used here.
9 J.L. Burckhardt, *Travels in Nubia* (London, 1813), 275.
10 F. Cailliaud, *Voyage à Méroe et au Fleuve Blanc* (Paris, 1823–27).

11 *Journal D'un Voyage à Méroe dans les Années 1821 et 1822.* (Khartoum, 1958). Linant was employed by the English antiquarian William Bankes, hence the reference in his graffito of having been *mandé par l'Angleterre.*

12 *SNR*, IX, Part 2 (1926), 59–67.

13 G.A.Hoskins, *Travels in Ethiopia* (London, 1835).

14 Ferlini's own account is given in *Cenno sugli Scavi Operati nella Nubia* (Bologna, 1837) and in a French translation with some variations as *Relation Historique de Fouilles opérées dans la Nubie* (Rome, 1838). The relevant parts of both versions are given in Budge (1907), 307–320.

15 *RCK*, I, II, III, IV, V.

16 MacIver (1909) and Woolley (1910).

17 MacAdam, (1949), (1955).

18 *Kush*, VII (1959), 171–196. *Kush*, X (1962), 170–202.

19 *Syria*, XXXIX (1962), 263–299.

CHAPTER II

1 *JEA*, 36 (1950), 36 ff.

2 Merowe, the modern administrative town approximately on the site of ancient Napata must be carefully distinguished from the ancient Meroe. Confusion between the two, owing to the coincidental (?) similarity of the names, has been a constant source of error.

3 *LAAA*, 10 (1923), 73–171.

4 Earlier writers, notably Reisner, used the term Ethiopia where Kush is now generally used. This was the term used by classical writers but because of confusion with the modern Ethiopia (Abyssinia) it is better not to use it.

5 *SNR*, 11 (1919), 41–44.

6 *RCK*, I, 2.

7 Arkell (1961), 110–137.

8 *RCK*, I.

9 *Harvard African Studies*, 11 (1918), 1–64. *RCK*, II.

10 *JEA*, 9 (1923), 75. *RCK*, V.

11 These two scholars have produced chronological schemes which show some variation. They are shown in tabular form on pp. 58–61.

12 *JEA*, 38 (1952), 75–77.

13 *BIFAO*, 50 (1952), 157–207.
14 Crowfoot (1911) gives an excellent and vivid description of the Butana region and its Meroitic sites.
15 *Chronique d'Egypte*, 53 (1952), 257–281.
16 J. W. Crowfoot, *Geographical Journal*, XXXVII (1911), 523–550, discusses the historical topography of this coast.
17 Hintze (1962), 13–19.
18 *JEA*, 9 (1923), loc. cit. *RCK*, IV, 2–8.
19 Hintze (1959) and modification in *Die Inschriften des Loewentempels von Musawwarat es Sofra*. (Berlin, 1962).
20 *Ghana Notes and Queries*, 3 (1961), 4.
21 Macadam (1949), 50–67.
22 Budge (1912), 117–139.
23 *RCK*, II, 222 n. I.
24 *SNR*, XXVI (1945), 5–36.
25 This is not absolutely the first appearance of iron in Kush since Taharqa's tomb contained one iron spearhead, originally wrapped in gold foil. *RCK*, II, 12.
26 Budge (1912), 140–169.
27 *JEA*, 33 (1947), 58–62 and *JEA*, 41 (1955), 128, 129.
28 Hintze (1959), 17–20 where the full argument is given.
29 Kienitz, *Die Politische Geschichte Aegyptens vom. 7. bis 4 Jahrhundert vor der Zeitwende* (Berlin, 1953), 185–199.
30 Macadam (1955), 20.
31 Macadam (1949), 90; (1955), Pl. XCI.
32 Detailed arguments are given in Hintze (1962), 13–19.
33 *LAAA*, 26 (1939–40), 3–9.
34 Arkell (1961), 159. *JEA*, 9 (1923), 42, 43.
35 *Kush* VIII (1960), 125–162. Now in Boston.
36 Meroe – Hamdab stela, *JEA*, 4 (1917), 159–173. Kawa – MacAdam (1949), 100 ff. Dakka – Griffith (1912). Pl. XII, XIII.
37 *JEA*, 4 (1917), 159–173. Monneret de Villard (1938), 11–15.
38 Macadam (1955), 22–23.
39 Geography, 17, 53, 54. Loeb translation.
40 *Nat. Hist.* VI, 181, 182. Loeb translation.
41 *Roman History*, LIV, 4, 5, Loeb translation.
42 *Journal of Roman History*, 40 (1950), 57 ff.

43 Now in the British Museum. For identification with Augustus see *LAAA*, 4 (1911), 66 ff.
44 *Loc. cit.*
45 *LAAA*, 5. (1912), 74.
46 Vercoutter, *Syria*, XXXIX, (1962), 263–299.
47 *Kush*, VII (1959), 178 and Griffith (1912), No. 46.
48 Hintze, *op. cit.*, 45.
49 Griffith, (1912), No. 129.
50 Griffith, (1911a), 72, No. 112.
51 Garstang (1911), 12–15.
52 Arkell (1961), 164.
53 Budge (1907), II, 126, 127.
54 *Kush*, VII (1959), 189–192.
55 L.P.Kirwan in review, *Antiquity*, 34 (1960), 69–70 suggests Meroe pyramids S. 3, S. 6, N. 8, and N. 13 are later than the accepted dates, basing his argument on Roman objects found in them.
56 Griffith, *Catalogue of the Demotic Graffiti of the Dodechacoenus* (Oxford, 1937), 114–119. Ph. 416.
57 *RCK*, IV, 3.
58 *Kush*, VIII (1960), 163–173. *Kush*, III (1955), 82–85.
59 The original is in Ethiopic and is published in *Deutsche Axum Expedition*, IV, 32–35. The latest translation is by Littmann in *Misc. Acad. Berol*, II, 2, 97–127. This English version is given by Kirwan, *Kush*, VIII (1960), 163–165, by whose permission it is reprinted here. For intelligibility the original lineation has been ignored.
60 *PSBA*, 31 (1909), 189, 190. The inscription itself is in Khartoum where it bears the number 508.
61 *Kush*, I (1953), 40–46.
62 *Kush*, II (1954), 66–85.
63 W.B.Emery and L.P.Kirwan, *The Royal Tombs of Ballana and Qustul* (Cairo, 1938).
64 Kirwan (1939).
65 *Kush*, V (1957), 37–41.

CHAPTER III

All sites which have inscriptions or reliefs are listed with a full bibliography in B. Porter and R. L. B. Moss, *Topographical Bibliography of Ancient*

Egyptian Hieroglyphic Texts, Reliefs and Paintings Volume VII (Oxford 1951). Information available there is not repeated.

1   The most northerly Meroitic site known is at Garba just south of Maharraqa. Firth, *Bulletin of the Archaeological Survey of Nubia,* No. 7, 11.

2   When the first Aswan dam was built a survey was carried out between 1907 and 1911 and published in a series of volumes of the *Archaeological Survey of Nubia*. A heightening of the dam caused a further survey to be made 1929–1931, published as W. B. Emery and L. P. Kirwan, *The Excavations and Survey Between Wadi es Sebua and Adindan* (Cairo, 1935). The building of the new dam has caused a great deal of archaeological activity during the last few years; though most of this work is as yet unpublished it does not seem to change the picture of the Meroitic period in Lower Nubia.

3   Emery and Kirwan, *op. cit.,* 23.

4   Firth, *loc. cit.*

5   Above p. 000.

6   G. Roeder, *Der Tempel Von Dakke,* 2 vols (Cairo, vol. 1 1930, vol. 2 1913).

7   Emery and Kirwan, *op. cit.,* 24.

8   A full list of sites from Wadi es Sebua to the Sudan frontier is given by Emery and Kirwan, *op. cit., passim.*

9   MacIver (1909), 23–42.

10   Woolley (1910).

11   B. Trigger, *Postilla,* 72 (1962), 1–12.

12   Emery and Kirwan, *op. cit.,* 417.

13   Faras is published in a series of articles by the excavator, F. Ll. Griffith, scattered through many volumes of *LAAA*. The specifically Meroitic parts are to be found in *LAAA*, XI (1924), 115–180, XII (1925) 57–172, XIII (1926) 17–37.

14   *JEA,* 11 (1925), 259–268.

15   *op. cit.*

16   A mastaba is a flat-topped superstructure like a truncated pyramid. The word is Arabic and means 'bench'.

17   *Kush,* XI (1963), 238–256.

18   *Kush,* X (1962), 10–75 *passim*, XI (1963), 138–9.

19   *Harvard African Studies,* VIII (1927), 1–121.

20 *Kush,* XI (1963), 24–28.
21 D. Dunham and J. Janssen *Second Cataract Forts,* I (Boston, 1960), 32.
22 A full bibliography of this and other sites is given in Porter and Moss *op. cit.*
23 Budge (1907), I, 467.
24 *JEA,* 22 (1936), 101, 102.
25 Lepsius, *Denkmäler,* I, Bl, 115.
26 Griffith (1912), 9–14.
27 Griffith, *op. cit.,* 11.
28 *JEA,* 33 (1947), 65.
29 MacAdam (1949) and (1955).
30 Now in the Ashmolean Museum.
31 *RCK,* I.
32 *RCK,* II.
33 In these parts there is frequent confusion in naming the points of the compass. Local convention is to regard the river as running from south to north and to orientate accordingly. Hence the left bank is always the west. Since at Nuri the river is in fact flowing north to south this causes east and west to be reversed in local speech, and Nuri will be described as being on the west bank, whereas in fact it is on the east. In this book the correct geographical sense is meant in all references to points of the compass.
34 I. E. S. Edwards, *The Pyramids of Egypt* (London, 1961), 196.
35 Edwards, *op. cit.,* 197–199, fig. 50.
36 *Kush,* XI (1963), 159–174.
37 *RCK,* I, 121–132.
38 *LAAA,* XI (1924), 72–124, and *LAAA,* X (1923), 73–171.
39 *JEA,* 4 (1917), 213–227, 5 (1918), 99–112, 6 (1920), 247–264.
40 Above p. 32.
41 Crowfoot (1911), 8, and *Kush,* I (1953), 8, 9.
42 Griffith (1911b) No. 74.
43 Perhaps connected with Nubian *Gel* 'Red'.
44 Crowfoot *loc. cit.* lists some of them.
45 *Kush,* VII (1959), 171–196, gives a preliminary report of the Butana expedition of the Humboldt University of Berlin in the course of which all Meroitic sites in the Butana were visited.

46 For reports from the second season onwards see, *LAAA* 4 (1912), 45–71, 5 (1913), 73–83, 6 (1914) 1–21, 7 (1914–16), 1–24.

47 *RCK,* IV and V.

48 J. Ward, *Our Sudan* (London, 1905), 156.

49 Garstang (1911), 26.

50 *op. cit.,* 25.

51 This block was removed to the Khartoum Museum. No. 5092. Another similar helmet is to be seen in the relief on the south wall of the forecourt of pyramid Beg. N.11.

52 *op. cit.,* 58 ff.

53 It was uncovered and the inscription copied by Hintze, *Kush,* VII (1959), 175. Published by Monneret de Villard, *ibid,* 111–113 and better by Hintze, *Kush* IX (1961), 279–282.

54 The error was first pointed out by Crowfoot, *SNR,* VII (2) (1924), 18–28 and amplified in Kirwan (1939), 41–42.

55 *Kush* I (1953), 40–46.

56 Kirwan (1939), 42.

57 *RCK,* IV and V contain full descriptions of all these burials.

58 The letters N, S, and W are used with numbers to designate the various burials. The system of numbering originally used by Reisner is now standard. The three main groups of burials are described as Ku (Kurru), Nu (Nuri), and Beg (Begarawiya = Meroe). The Beg cemeteries are subdivided as above. Thus Beg. N. 1. means tomb. One of the North Cemetery at Meroe.

59 *SNR,* XXVIII (1947), 7–9.

60 Lepsius, *Denkmäler,* Plates I, 139a, 141. Text V, 335.

61 *Syria,* XXXIX (1962), 263–299.

62 *Kush,* VII, (1959), 171–196, gives a list.

63 For this and other suggestions of Indian influence see A. J. Arkell, *Meroe and India* in *Aspects of Archaeology in Britain and Beyond,* ed. Grimes (London 1951), 32–38. A later note by Vychicl, *Kush* VI (1958), 174–176 does not take note of Arkell.

64 Hintze (1959), 36–39.

65 *Kush,* VII (1959), 187.

66 These were mostly published by Lepsius and have been re-examined by Hintze. A full bibliography is given in Porter and Moss (1951) VII, 264–267 and additional material in *Kush* VII (1959), 180–183.

67 P.L.Shinnie, *Kush* IX (1961), 284–286, and F.Hintze, *Kush*, XII (1964), 296–298.

68 *Kush*, X (1962), 170–202; *Kush*, XI (1963), 217–226.

69 Hintze (1962).

70 For a discussion of the chronological problems see above p. 32.

71 From the Arabic root meaning 'to dig'.

72 Crowfoot (1911), 11–18.

73 *op. cit.*, Pl. VII.

74 *op. cit.*, Pl. XIII.

75 Porter and Moss (1951), VII, 272.

76 *Kush*, VII (1959), 189–192.

77 Crawford (1953), 36–39.

78 For details of its vicissitudes see P.L.Shinnie, *Excavations at Soba*, (Khartoum, 1955), 17.

79 The inscription is published in Griffith (1911b), 51–53.

80 *Antiquity*, 22 (1948), 8–12.

81 *Kush*, XI (1963), 227–234.

82 *Kush*, IV (1956), 4–18.

83 *Annales d'Ethiopie*, I (1955), 41.

CHAPTER IV

1 *JEA*, 50 (1964), 116.

2 *RCK*, V, 447 and figs. 242, 243, and fig. 27 in this work.

3 *JEA*, 33 (1947), 63–65.

4 *Kush*, I (1953), 53.

5 Garstang (1911), 19.

6 C.Aldred personal communication 13.7.60.

7 In the collections of the Wellcome Historical Medical Museum. *Kush*, XII (1964), 119–125.

8 *Journal of Hellenic Studies*, 35 (1915), 12–21. *American Journal of Archaeology*, 50 (1946), 217–240.

9 And not basalt as Garstang (1911), 22, suggests.

10 *Kush*, VIII (1960), 77–87. *Kush*, X, (1962), 335.

11 *Syria*, XXXIX (1962), 299. But if from China it should surely have two humps.

12 *Kush*, VII (1959), 91–92.

13 A.W.Lawrence, personal communication 8.8.60.

13a Macadam, Bulletin of the Allen Memorial Art Museum, XXIII (1966), 42–71 describes a gold stand of Queen Nawidemak which may go with this statuette.

14 Griffith in Garstang (1911), 62–63.

15 *JEA*, 4 (1917), 21–24.

16 If this is so either our date for Netekamani is wrong or the Arikan‑kharer of this piece is not the son shown with him several times, but another and later carrier of the same name.

17 Hintze (1959), 37–39.

18 A.J.Arkell, *Early Khartoum* (London, 1949). Plate 104, 105.

19 *Kush,* X (1962), 336–337.

20 *Syria,* XXXIX (1962), 298.

21 A bibliography is given by Adams, *Kush,* XII (1964), 173.

22 For a study of the Christian pottery see *Kush,* X (1962), 245–288.

23 *Kush,* XII (1964), 126–173.

24 *loc. cit.*

25 R.J.Charleston, *Roman Pottery* (London, 1955), 36–37.

26 *op. cit.* Plate 56.

27 *RCK,* V, 383.

28 A description of modern pot making is given in P.L.Shinnie, *Excavations at Soba* (Khartoum, 1961), 81–82.

29 Budge (1907), I, 285–307.

30 Most of the Ferlini collection is now in Berlin, some in Munich.

31 So called in the publication. It is probable that they are of microcline (Amazon stone). See A.Lucas and J.R.Harris, *Ancient Egyptian Materials and Industries,* (London, 1962), 390.

32 Illustrated in *RCK* II, Plate CXVI.

33 Examples are illustrated in *LAAA,* XI (1924), Plates LIII, LIV.

34 *Kush,* XI (1963), Plates XXXI, XLVIII.

35 *Harvard African Studies,* VIII, Plate XXXI.

36 It was found in the Boston Expedition house at Giza in Egypt. It is not listed in any of the excavation records but certainly came from one of the Meroitic royal cemeteries. It is now in Khartoum. See *RCK,* V, 447.

37 Woolley (1910), 59–60.

38 D.Dunham, *The Egyptian Department and its Excavations* (Boston, 1958), 130.

39 *Loc. cit.*
40 Woolley (1910), 74.
41 J.D.Cooney, *Journal of Glass Studies,* II (1960), 29.
42 D.B.Harden, *Roman Glass from Karanis* (Ann Arbor, 1936), 39.
43 Grave 2097, see *LAAA,* XII (1925), 148.
44 Further illustrations can be seen in Woolley, *op. cit.,* Plates 37–39.
45 Karanis Glass XII, Group A.Harden, *op. cit.,* 252–254.
46 Harden, *op. cit.,* 265.
47 Karanis Glass XIII, Type A.
48 *RCK,* IV, 149–151.
49 Karanis Glass XIII, Type B.
50 Garstang (1911), Plate XXXVII.

CHAPTER V

1 F.C.Gau, *Antiquités de la Nubie* (Stuttgart and Paris, 1821–27), Plate XIV, No. 44.
2 For a discussion of the linguistic position of Nubian see C.H.Armbruster, *Grammar of Dongolese Nubian* (Cambridge, 1960), 13–35.
3 F.Ll.Griffith in MacIver (1909) 43–54, and Griffith (1911).
4 E.Zyhlarz,'Das Meroitishe Sprachproblem', *Anthropos,* XXV (1930) 409–463.
5 F.Hintze, *Die Sprachliche Stellung des Meroitischen* (Berlin, 1955).
6 J.H.Greenberg, *Studies in African Linguistic Classification* (New Haven, 1955), 98.
7 For these languages see *SNR,* XXI (1958), 122–165.
8 *Kush,* XII (1964), 188–194. See also *Journal of African History,* VII (1966), 19–25.
9 For a classification and list of these languages see J.H.Greenberg, *Languages of Africa* (The Hague, 1963), 83–129.
10 Griffith in MacIver, *op. cit.,* 43–54.
11 *Denkmäler,* V, 55a and Griffith (1911b), No. 41.
12 Griffith (1911), 7.
13 Demotic is the late form of Egyptian written in a very abbreviated form.
14 For publication of these and the arguments for the interpretation see Griffith (1911), 29–53.
15 Hintze (1959), 11–16.

16 Karanog inscription no. 96.
17 Hintze (1959), 14.
18 Ancient Egyptian belongs to the family of Afro-Asiatic languages, amongst the best-known living examples of which are Arabic, Hebrew, Hausa and Berber. None of these is very close to Egyptian but even had Coptic, the latest form of Egyptian, not been known some idea of Egyptian could have been obtained by comparison with these languages.

CHAPTER VI

1 This is the only place in which the name of this god is known to us written in hieroglyphs. All other mentions are in Meroitic cursive. It is interesting to note that the Meroitic sound we transliterate as *d* was heard by the Egyptians as *r* and is so written.
2 Hintze (1962), 19–21. The identification of Musawwarat seems fairly certain from the many references to it in the texts there; that of Wad ben Naqa rather less so.
3 The Meroitic place name *twylkt* seems to be that of Naqa. Hintze *op. cit.,* 20–21.
4 A free translation from the version in Hintze (1962), 28.
5 Griffith (1911b), 57–60.
6 Monneret de Villard, *Rassegna di Studi Etiopici,* Anno II, Num. II, 107–142.
7 *Op. cit.,* 114–124.
8 *Syria,* XXXIX (1962), fig. 14.
9 M. de Villard, *op. cit.,* 108.
10 Monneret de Villard suggests the name may be connected with the Old Nubian word meaning 'sun'.
11 G. A. Reisner, *Excavations at Kerma,* parts I–III and IV–V (Harvard African Studies, V and VI) Cambridge, Mass., 1923.
12 *Shawabtis* are small models of mummified bodies, usually made of faience, which were placed in Egyptian tombs in large numbers. They were intended to carry out various manual tasks for the deceased in the after-life.
13 *RCK,* V, 28–39.
14 *op. cit.,* 44–46.
15 At Karanog 783 graves were listed, and at Faras 2,990.

16 For exceptions see Woolley (1910), 26.
17 For a reconstruction of a tomb see *op. cit.* Plate 114.

CHAPTER VII

1 MacAdam (1949).
2 The painting of the queen mother at Faras is evidence of this. *Kush* XII (1964), Plate XLIIb.
3 *JEA*, 50 (1964), 130–131.
4 Woolley (1910), 4.
5 *RCK*, IV, 143–144.
6 *Kush*, IV (1956), 86–87.
7 Arabic *kohl* from which the pots are usually known as *kohl* pots.
8 *Kush*, XI (1963), 26.
9 *Harvard African Studies*, VI (1923), 208–220.
10 Beg. W. 415.
11 *RCK*, IV, 149 and fig. 98.
12 Woolley, *op. cit.*, Plates 21, 22, 26.
13 *RCK*, IV, Plate LXXI.
14 *RCK*, IV, 92.
15 Very few certain remains of horses were found in the Meroe royal cemeteries and there is some uncertainty in a number of cases as to whether animal bones found were horse or ox.
16 Strabo, 17.
17 Arkell (1961), 166.
18 For a description of this see H. Sassoon, *Bulletin of the South African Archaeological Society*, XVIII (1963), 176–180.
19 An iron spearhead in the tomb of Taharqa pre-dates this but it is an isolated piece and was regarded as so valuable that it was wrapped in gold leaf.
20 A detailed study of the introduction of iron in Napatan and Meroitic times has been made by G. A. Wainwright, *SNR*, 26 (1945), 5–36.
21 Mounds of iron slag are known for example from Kerma, Kawa, and Argo.
22 Arkell (1961), 151.
23 In grave W.122, *RCK*, V, 205–206.
24 Arkell, *op. cit.*, 174.

25 Examples have been found at Ain Fara, *Kush,* VII (1959), 115–119, as well as at Koro Toro in the Republic of Chad, *Kush,* XI (1963), 315–319.

26 For these Bornu buildings and their possible contact with the Nile see *Journal of African History,* III (1962), 1–10.

27 Shinnie, 'The Legacy of Egypt to Africa', in *Legacy of Egypt* (in press).

28 For detailed references see Shinnie, *op. cit.*

29 The Bronze Age, such an important stage in human development in Europe and Asia, has no place in Africa except in such parts of the northern half of the continent as were in touch with the Bronze Age cultures of the Near East and the Mediterranean.

30 See Carbon 14 dates collected by B.M.Fagan and published in *Journal of African History,* II (1961), 137–139; IV (1963), 127–128; VI (1965), 107–116.

31 For a survey of the evidence see Huard, *Bulletin de l'Institut Français d'Afrique Noire,* XXII, B (1960) 134–178 and XXVI, B (1964), 297–395.

32 The view that the organisation of the states of the western Sudan was ultimately derived from Meroe is ably presented in R. Oliver and J.D.Fage, *A Short History of Africa,* London 1962, 49–50.

Bibliography

An almost complete bibliography, by Fawzi Gadallah, appeared in *Kush*, XI (1963), 207–216 and need not be repeated here. Two major works have been since published, namely:

D.Dunham, *Royal Cemeteries of Kush*, V; *The West and South Cemeteries at Meroe* (Boston, 1963).

F.Hintze, *Die Inschriften des Löwentempels von Musawwarat es Sofra.* (Berlin, 1962).

Since so few specialized studies of Meroitic culture have been published most of the material in this book has been extracted from excavation reports to which detailed references are given in the text.

Sources of Illustrations

The photographs for Plates 2, 7, 9, 13, 14, 18, 19, 20, 21, 32, 34, 35, 38, 54, 64, 66, 67, 70, 71, 74, 77, 82, 84 are the author's own. Acknowledgement is also made to the following:
Ashmolean Museum, Oxford: 37, 39–53, 55–59, 62, 63, 68, 73, 75, 76, 83; Trustees of the British Museum: 28, 36, 65; Museum of Fine Arts, Boston: 60, 61, 69, 72, 78–81; Ny Carlsberg Glyptotek, Copenhagen: 24, 25; The Oriental Institute, The University of Chicago: 1, 8, 10–12, 15–17, 22, 23; The University of Liverpool, School of Archaeology and Oriental Studies: 3, 4–6, 26, 27; The Walters Art Gallery, Baltimore: 31; Worcester Art Museum, Worcester, Mass: 33; Professor J. Vercoutter: 29, 30: The line drawings are from a wide variety of sources acknowledged in the captions. Figs. 1, 2, 8, 10 and 16 were drawn by Mr H. A. Shelley, figs. 12, 14, 19–21, 28, 29, 40 and 41 by Miss Lucinda Rodd, and figs. 4–6, 9, 11, 13, 17, 18, 22, 37–39, 42–54, 56–63 by Mrs Shinnie.

6

7

8

9

10

11

12

15

16

17

18

19

20

21

22

23

4

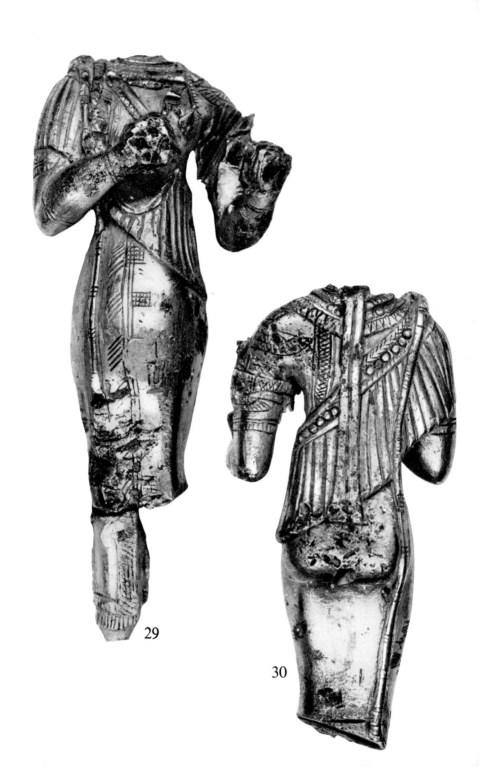

29

30

31

32

33

34

35

36

37

38

39 40 41

42

43

44

45

46

47

48

49

50

51

52

53

54

55

56

57

58   59

61

62

63

65

66

67   68

69

70

71

72   73

75

74

76

78

79

80

81

82

83

84

Notes on the Plates

1   Pyramid N.22 at Meroe. The pyramid of King Netekamani with ruins of chapel and pylons at the front. Note the small sandstone blocks of which the pyramid is constructed.

2   The pyramids of Meroe. The northern group of pyramids seen from the south.

3   Temple of Amun at Meroe from the west, during the excavation in 1910. The main part of the town can be seen in the background. The figure stands in the Hall of Columns and in front of the dais.

4   The Kiosk at Meroe standing in front of the temple of Amun and viewed from that temple, during the 1910 excavations. The granite rams line the approach to the temple.

5   Steps approaching the sanctuary of the Sun Temple at Meroe. Traces of relief can be seen on the wall to the right.

6   The sanctuary of the Sun Temple at Meroe. The circular arrangement is part of the blue glazed tiling which completely covered the floor and was so laid out by the excavator.

7   The hypostyle of the palace, Wad ben Naqa. This hypostyle was on the southern side of the palace and the main entrance opened into it. The six columns, of which five are visible, were of sandstone, the walls of the palace of brick.

8   Naqa. The Lion Temple. The nearer pylon has a relief of Queen Amanitare holding a group of enemies in the right hand and, in her left, a sword with which she is about to strike them. The side wall bears reliefs of the royal family standing before a procession of gods.

9   Storeroom in the palace, Wad ben Naqa. The pots stored here cannot have contained anything, as many of them were placed mouth down.

10, 11 Reliefs on the back wall of the Lion Temple at Naqa. The multi-faced and armed representation of the Lion-god may be due to Indian influence. King Netekamani and his queen, Amanitare, are standing before the god and behind each of them is a prince.

12 The Lion-god Apedemek with the body of a snake emerging from a flower, on the side of the north pylon of the Lion Temple, Naqa. This representation may also show Indian influence. To the left can just be seen Queen Amanitare followed by a prince.

13 The Kiosk at Naqa. This small temple shows Roman influence in the capitals and rounded arches, whilst the lintel in the centre is purely Egyptian. This mixture of styles is characteristic of buildings of the Roman period in Egypt.

14 Closer view of part of the Kiosk at Naqa showing both Roman capitals and an Egyptian-style frieze of cobras bearing the sun disk (*uraei*) as well as the winged sun disk.

15 Entrance to Temple F at Naqa. This temple bears the name of Queen Shanakdakhete and is the oldest temple at Naqa.

16 Ram of granite, Naqa. These representations of rams, the animal sacred to the god Amun, are common in Meroitic times and frequently line the approach to a temple. Compare those at Meroe in Plate 4.

17 Musawwarat es-Sofra. View of the temple at the centre of the main complex. This temple stands well above the other buildings and earlier ones have been found beneath it. This photograph was taken before the recent clearing and excavation.

18 Musawwarat es-Sofra. Columns of the north colonnade of the central temple, after clearing.

19 Musawwarat es-Sofra, entrance to the North-East Temple with colossal figures on either side of the doorway. The inner jambs of the doorway have representations of a snake similar to that in Plate 12 from Naqa, and

between the jambs and the giant figures the foreparts of two lions project from the wall.

20 Musawwarat es-Sofra. Termination of wall in main complex in the form of an elephant. This is a unique piece of sculpture and indicates the very special importance of the elephant at this site.

21 Fragmentary statue from Meroe of ferricrete sandstone. This statue prob-ably dates from about the time of Netekamani and presumably stood at the entrance of one of the temples. This fragment is still on the site.

22 Column drum from Musawwarat es-Sofra showing a number of gods. The high relief is unusual, although there are several examples at this site, and, decayed as they are, they are strongly reminiscent of some Indian sculpture.

23 Colossal granite statue of Netekamani (?) at Hag Zummar, Argo Island. This statue and the similar broken one which lies beside it originally stood in front of a temple. The identification with Netekamani is based on stylistic considerations. There are many points of resemblance to the statuary of Hellenistic Egypt, particularly in the fillet of leaves around the crown. The necklace of large beads is similar to ones in the reliefs at Naqa.

24 Colossal statue of sandstone found at a low level in the mound known as the Temple of Isis at Meroe. This statue must, like all the foregoing, have stood at the entrance to a temple. Ht. 2.23 m. Ny Carlsberg Glyptothek, Copenhagen, AEIN 1082.

25 Plaster statue from Meroe. This statue was found in the bath and rep-resents a man reclining in a restful attitude appropriate to one in a bath house. It shows Hellenistic influence. Max. ht. 80 cm. Ny Carlsberg Glyptothek, Copenhagen, AEIN 1484.

26, 27 Pair of plaster statues from Meroe. They were found in the corner of building No. 295. The male figure is of a dark red colour, whilst the female is yellow, thus maintaining the colour differentiation between the sexes familiar from Egyptian art. Life-size. Khartoum Museum.

28 Roman head in bronze. This is almost certainly a representation of the Emperor Augustus. It was found at Meroe in front of temple No. 292 in a pocket of clean sand. Ht. 48.25 cm. British Museum.

29, 30 Gold figurine of a queen found on a tip heap near the Barkal temples. From the regalia it is probably to be dated to the end of the first century BC. Ht. 10 cm. Khartoum Museum, No. 5457.

31 Plaque of dark red slate from the Lion Temple at Meroe. The two pieces are the back and front of what was originally one, the plaque having split anciently into two. The left-hand portion shows King Tanyidamani and the right-hand one the Lion-god Apedemek. It dates from the late second century BC. Ht. 17.7 cm. Walters Art Gallery, Baltimore, No. 22.258.

32 Steatite stela from Amun Temple, Meroe. It shows a king on the left before the ram-headed god Amun, and on the right a queen before the goddess Isis. Khartoum Museum, No. 522.

33 Sandstone plaque showing Prince Arikhankharer slaying his enemies. Probably from Meroe. Possibly second century AD. Ht. 21.2 cm. Worcester Art Museum, Worcester, Mass. No. 1922.145.

34, 35 Bronze figurine of a king (or god?) wearing the double crown of Egypt with an unusual type of wreath round his head. Possibly first century AD. From Kawa Temple T. Ht. 20.2 cm. Khartoum Museum, No. 2715.

36 Bronze head of a goddess (?) with cartouche of Arnekhamani. From Kawa, Temple A. Over-all ht. 17.5 cm. British Museum, 63585.

37 Sandstone head of a Ba statue from Faras, Grave 5202. Ashmolean Museum. No. 1912.456.

38 One of a pair of bronze heads of the god Dionysus of Greek workmanship and Hellenistic date. From Meroe, pyramid N. 5. The other of the pair is in Boston. The band round the hair is inlaid with silver. Ht. 12 cm. Khartoum Museum, No. 1948.

39-41   Painted pottery cups with zoomorphic designs. Faras. Ht. 8 and 7 cm. resp. Ashmolean Museum, Nos. 1912.308, 401, 405.

42   Incised and painted pot. Faras, grave 2710. Diam. 14.2 cm. Ashmolean Museum, No. 1912.481.

43   Pots. The two outer ones painted, the centre one impressed with designs imitating Roman *terra sigillata*. Faras. Ht. of centre pot 9 cm. Ashmolean Museum, Nos. 1912. 393, 688, 339.

44, 45   Two painted pots showing human figures in caricature. Faras, from graves 701A and 2055, respectively. Ht. 21 and 25 cm. resp. Ashmolean Museum, Nos. 1912. 322, 445.

46   Painted pot showing lion eating a man. The man has three vertical scars on his cheek similar to ones still to be seen in the Sudan. Faras. Ashmolean Museum, No. 1912.324.

47   Painted pot with heads of the Lion-god Apedemek, and *uraei*. Faras, grave 1090. Ht. 12.5 cm. Ashmolean Museum, No. 1912.410.

48   Red-ware pot painted with band showing seated frogs with plants between them. Faras. Ht. 25 cm. Ashmolean Museum, No. 1912.332.

49, 50   Two red-ware painted pots, the left-hand one with faces, the right-hand one with plain bands. Faras, graves 974, 932. Ht. 20 and 21 cm. resp. Ashmolean Museum, Nos. 1912.370, 333.

51   Painted jug with a design similar to fish scales on a cream-coloured body. Faras, grave 2912. Ht. 18.5 cm. Ashmolean Museum, No. 1912.500.

52   Three pots. The two outer ones painted, the centre one burnished black with incised white-filled decoration. Faras, graves 974/2, 2372/1, 2912/5. Ht. of centre pot 11 cm. Ashmolean Museum, Nos. 1912. 369, 814, 501.

53   Two pots with raised barbotine decoration of Roman type. Faras, graves 2718, 2099. Ashmolean Museum, Nos. 1912.485, 745. Ht. of r.h. pot 9.5 cm.

54 Pot with raised barbotine decoration. Meroe. Khartoum Museum. Ht. 7 cm.

55 Three pots. The left-hand one with raised barbotine decoration, the centre one painted with a checkerboard pattern on the neck, the right-hand one of black ware impressed and red-filled. Faras, graves 2819, 2006, 972. Ht. of centre pot 12 cm. Ashmolean Museum, Nos. 1912.491, 775, 366.

56 Highly burnished black-ware pots, two with impressed white-filled decoration. Faras, West Palace. Ht. of centre pot 8.6 cm. Ashmolean Museum, No. 1912.895, 896,897.

57 Black burnished pot with impressed white-filled decoration. Faras. Ashmolean Museum, No. 1912.733.

58 Large 'beer' pot with impressed decoration. These impressed tassels are a favourite decorative motif. Faras. Ashmolean Museum, No. 1912.464.

59 Large black-ware pot with impressed decoration. Faras, grave 2642A. Ht. 26 cm. Ashmolean Museum, No. 1912.687.

60 Gold jewellery. The top six pieces are earrings, four of them consisting of heads of the goddess Hathor with rosettes and pendants. The two lower pieces are bracelets, consisting of gold and carnelian beads enclosed by gold wire. Meroe, pyramid W.5. Museum of Fine Arts, Boston, Mass.

61 Gold rings. They mostly bear engraved designs of Egyptian deities, but the centre one of the top row has the Greek words H XAPIC, and the left-hand one of the bottom row has an agate with an intaglio figure of the goddess Athena. All from the West Cemetery at Meroe. Museum of Fine Arts, Boston, Mass.

62 Two gold amulets, one representing a fly, the other a cowrie shell. Faras, grave 2782. Ashmolean Museum, No. 1912.671, 673.

63 Beads from tomb 1155 at Faras. The upper string has droplet beads of

quartz together with two small ones of glass. The lower string consists of carnelian beads with faience amulets as spacers. Ashmolean Museum, Nos. 1912.369, 814, 501.

64 Bronze bowl engraved with design of baskets of fruit. Meroe, grave W308. Ht. 8 cm. Khartoum Museum, No. 2145.

65 Bronze bowl with engraved *uraei* round the rim and *ankh* signs on the body. Faras. Ht. 9.5 cm. British Museum, 51461.

66 Bronze bowl with foot and handles. Gemai, cemetery 100, grave E.99. Khartoum Museum, No. 1505.

67 Bronze beaker decorated with parallel engraved lines. Meroe, grave W308. Ht. 9.8 cm. Khartoum Museum, No. 2146.

68 Bronze bottle with separate lid. Faras. Ht. with lid 11.5 cm. Ashmolean Museum, Nos. 1912.891, 892.

69 Bronze lamp with iron stem and bronze hook, and flame-guard in shape of an acanthus leaf. The iron stem is a modern restoration. Meroe, tomb N. 29, that of King Takideamani. Over-all ht. 23 cm. Museum of Fine Arts, Boston, Mass. No. 24. 959.

70 Bronze lamp with handle in form of a centaur. Meroe, tomb N. 18. Over-all ht. 19 cm. Khartoum Museum, No. 1826.

71 Bronze lamp with two elephant-heads. Meroe, tomb W.102. Khartoum Museum, No. 1947.

72 Bronze lamp with handle in form of the forepart of a horse. Meroe, tomb N.18, that of Amanikhatashan. Over-all ht. 22 cm. Museum of Fine Arts, Boston, Mass. No. 24.967.

73 Bronze lamp. Faras, grave 151. Ashmolean Museum, No. 1912.292.

74   Silver porringer with two large handles and decoration of wavy lines in relief. The two handles have designs, which may be owner's marks, scratched on them. Meroe, tomb N.18. Diam. 22 cm. Khartoum Museum, No. 1827.

75, 76   Bronze mirror cover. On the outside is an applied female head also in bronze, of Hellenistic style. The inside shows Harpocrates on a lotus surrounded by mythical and other animals of Oriental style. Faras, grave 2589. Diam. 20 cm. Ashmolean Museum, No. 1912.460.

77   Bronze hanging vase in shape of boy's head. The eyes are inlaid in silver. The handles terminate in loops in the shape of ducks' heads. Second – third centuries AD. Faras, grave 71. Over-all ht. 11.5 cm. Khartoum Museum, No. 693.

78–81   Silver goblet, originally gilded, with scene in relief. Probably Roman work of about the middle of the first century AD. Found amongst fallen blocks of tomb N. 2 at Meroe. Museum of Fine Arts, Boston, Mass. No. 24.971.

82   Oil flask, in green blown glass. It dates from the mid third to the mid fourth century AD and was probably made in Egypt. Faras, grave 1203. Ht. 7.5 cm. Khartoum Museum, No. 699.

83   Moulded glass beaker. Probably made in Egypt in the first or second century AD. Faras, grave 2097. Ht. 12 cm. Ashmolean Museum, No. 1912.1137.

84   Blown glass *unguentarium* of brown/purple colour with yellow threads. Probably made in Egypt between AD 200 and 400. Meroe, grave 300. Ht. 9.8 cm. Khartoum Museum. No. 525.

Index

Abratoi, 52

Abu Simbel, Greek and Carian inscriptions at, 32, 64

Adams, W. Y., cited, 117

Addison, F., cited, 98

Aelius Gallus, 18

Aezanes inscription, 52, 57

agriculture, 158ff.

Akinidad, 42; inscription at Meroe, 43ff.,
81; at Kawa, 48, 70; Sun Temple, 83;
Hamdab stela, 84

Aksha, cemetery, 67

Alwa (Soba), 57, 97

Amanikhabale, at Meroe, 48; at Basa, 48,
95; bronze cone from Kawa, 127

Amanikhatashan, 128

Amani-Nataki-Lebte, 81

Amani-Nete-Yerike, 32; inscription at
Kawa, 37, 70

Amanirenas, name at Kawa, 20, 43; at
Dakka, 43; at Meroe, 43ff.; Hambab
stela, 84

Amanishakhete, 50; name at Kawa, 48,
70; at Dakka, 49; jewellery, 122

Amanislo, name at Barkal, 40; at Semna,
67, pyramid, 86

Amanitare, 49; monuments erected, 50;
name at Amara, 68; at Meroe 77, 81; at
Naqa, 88, 90; at Wat ben Naqa, 134

Amanitenmemide, 154

Amara, temple at, 67

Amtalqa, 31; name at Meroe, 81; gold
plaque, 123

Amun, Temple of, (Meroe), 20, 43; description, 77f.

animals, domestic, 159

Anlamani, 36; statue at Barkal, 74

antimony, 155

Apedemek, temple at Kawa, 70; stela in
Lion Temple, Meroe, 83; at Naqa, 88,
89; at Musawwarat, 94; reliefs from
Meroe, 105; from Musawwarat, 110;
from Naqa, 113; the god, 141, 142;
prayer to, 143

Apis, shrine of, 84

Arakakamani, first buried at Meroe, 32,
39, 40, 86; date of reign, 41

Argin, cemetery, 67

Argo Island, colossal statues on, 68, 101

Arikakhatani, at Naqa, 50, 91

Arikhankharer, at Naqa, 50, 89; sandstone plaque, 105

Arnekhamani, name at Musawwarat, 40;
at Kawa, 69, 104; and Ptolemy IV, 41;
reliefs, 110

Arqamani, reign of, 35, 41; chapel at
Dakka, 63; reliefs, 107

art, 99ff.; representations of elephants, 20,
100; of lions, 100; foreign influences,
100, 145

Aryamani, stela at Kawa, 69

'Asmach' (Egyptian deserters), 15, 19

Aspelta, name at Nuri, Meroe, 31; statue
at Barkal, 32, 74; reign, 35; shrine at
Kawa, 69; name at Napata, 73; at Barkal, 73; stela in Sun Temple, 83, 108

225

Assyrians, introduction of iron, 161
Aswan (Syene), 13, 18
Augustus, Emperor, 47; head of statue, 48, 79, 104
Axum, 52, 96

Ballana, 56
Barkal, Jebel, visited by Hoskins, 27, 29; broken statues at, 32, 74; description of site, 73ff.
Bartare, burial in South Cemetery, 40, 86
Basa, 48; description of site, 95; lion statues, 103, 145
beads, 125
Bellefonds, Linant de, cited, 25
bells, 129
Bini, 167
bronze, bowls from Axum, 97; small sculpture from Kawa, 104; head of Augustus, 104; grave goods, 126; lamps 127; bells, 129; tools, 162; cire-perdue casting, 167
Bruce, James, cited, 24, 75
Budge, Sir E.A. Wallis, 67, 76
buildings, domestic, 67, 156
Burckhardt, J.L., cited, 24
burial customs, 146ff.; bed burials, 148; coffin burials, 148; multiple burials, 150
Butana, the, description of, 33, 75

Cailliaud, F., cited, 25
Cambyses, 15, 19, 32, 39
Candace, 19, 20, 49
cemeteries, at Kurru, 70; at Nuri, 70ff.; at Barkal, 74; at Meroe, 85ff.
Christianity, introduction of, to Nubia, 57; evidence for Christian occupation at

Meroe, 80, 84; westward movement, 166
chronology of rulers, 29ff.; table 58–61
classical influences on pottery, 116ff.; jewellery, 124; metal ware, 127, 129
cloth, 152, 159
Crowfoot, J.W., 95

daily life, 153ff.
Dakka, inscriptions, 42, 43, 49; limit of Meroitic occupation, 62
Dangeil, description of site, 74
Dio Cassius, cited, 20, 47
Diocletian, 56
Diodorus Siculus, cited, 16, 32, 41
Dunham, Dows, cited, 27; chronology of rulers, 32, 36, 42, 43; typology of pyramids, 72; Argo colossi, 101; lamps, 128

eastern influences on Meroitic art, 100; Persian, 105; Indian, 111, 113, 159
Egypt, occupation of Nubia, 29, 42; influence on art and culture, 29, 99, 106, 107; on religion, 141ff.; on burial customs, 148
elephants in Meroitic art, 100, 101, 111, 127, 128; in religious cult, 146
Emery, W.B., cited, 63
Ergamenes, 18, 41

Faras, 49; Meroitic cemetery at, 64ff.; 'western palace', 66; town wall, 66; grave goods, 126, 129; glass, 130; burials, 151
Ferlini, 27, 75, 122
Firka, 57
food crops, 159

Fura, 97
furniture, 157

Gaius Petronius, 19, 20
Gaminarti, domestic building, 67
Garstang, J., 16; excavations at Meroe, 27, 75, 79, 102
Gemai, cemetery at, 67, 126
glass, 85, 130
gods, 142ff.
gold, statuette from Barkal, 105; plaques from Meroe, 123; jewellery, 122ff.
grammar, 139
grave goods, 152
grave types, 65
'Great Enclosure', Musawwarat, 93
Greek alphabet, 23
Greenberg, J.M., cited, 133
Griffith, F. Ll., excavations at Faras, 28, 64, 105; reading of Meroitic, 132, 138; inscriptions from Areika, 134

hafirs, 95
Hamdab stela, 81
Harsiotef, inscriptions, 37, 38; building at Kawa, 69; at Barkal, 73; iron in foundation deposits of pyramid, 161f.
Hatra, 96
Heliodorus, *Aethiopica* of, cited, 22
Hellenistic imports, bronze heads of Dionysus from Meroe, 104; pottery, 120, 122; jewellery, 124; metal ware, 127; glass, 130
Herodotus, cited, 13ff., 32, 81, 146, 165
Hintze, F., 21; chronology, 32, 35, 39, 40–43, 97; Meroitic language, 133, 138
Hoskins, G.A., cited, 26

Ife, 101, 167
iron, iron-working, 160; tools, 162; introduction of, to Central Africa, 168
irrigation, 160
Isis, Temple of, (Meroe), 80; description of, 84; statues, 102
Ismail Pasha, expedition to Sudan, 25

jewellery, 122ff.
Juvenal, cited, 22

Karanog, 49, 64; bronze bowl from, 126; bronze bell, 129; glass, 131; burials, 152
Kashta, 30
Kawa, 20, 28; inscriptions, 37; royal names, 39, 48, 49; details of site, 69ff.; bronze statuettes, 104; bronze cone, 127
Khabbash, 39
Kirwan, L.P., cited, 63
Kurru, 30, 70, 147

lamps, 127
language, 132ff.
Latin inscription (Musawwarat), 23, 94
Lepsius, C.R., visit to Sudan, 27; Amara temple, 68; Naqa, 88; collection of inscriptions, 132, 134
lion, in Meroitic art, 100; statues from Meroe and Basa, 103; in religion, 142
Lion Temple, Meroe, 83
Lion Temple, Musawwarat, 94; reliefs, 109, 412
Lion Temple, Naqa, 88; reliefs, 111

Macadam, M.F.L., cited, 39
MacIver, D.R., excavations at Areika and Karanog, 28

Maharraqa (Hiera Sycaminos), 50, 63

Malenaqen, 31; at Meroe, 81; gold plaque, 123

Malewiebamani, 73

Meroe, city of, seen by Bruce, 24; description by Burckhardt, 24f.; by Cailliaud, 25; by Linant de Bellefonds, 26; date of move to, 31; rainfall, 33; first mention of, 37; description of site, 75ff.; Temple of Amun, 77f.; royal city, 78ff.; evidence for occupation in Christian period, 80; Sun Temple, 81ff.; reliefs, 108f.; Lion Temple, 83f.; cemeteries, 85ff., 148ff.; iron working, 160ff.

Meroe, state of, discovery of, 13ff.; Island of, 16, 57, 95; contacts with Romans, 19, 20, 50; missions to Rome, 23, 48; decline and end of, 52ff.; geography of, 62ff.; organization of, 153; and Africa, 165

metal ware, 126

Moya, Jebel, 98

mummification, 148f.

Musawwarat es-Sofra, Latin inscription, 23; visited by Cailliaud, 25; by Linant de Bellefonds, 26; by Hoskins, 26, 34, 87; description of site, 92ff.; 'Great Enclosure', 93; Lion Temple, 94; statues, 102; elephants at, 146

Naldamek, 42, 74

Napata, 29ff.; move of capital from, 31, 37; site of, 73

Naqa, visited by Cailliaud, 25; by Linant de Bellefonds, 26; by Lepsius, 87; description of site, 88ff.; statues, 102; reliefs, 111

Naqa, Wad ben, visited by Hoskins, 26, 48, 50; description of site, 87ff; inscription from, 134ff.

Nastasen, reign of, 33, 37; inscription at Barkal, 38; burial at Nuri, 72, 97

Nero, Emperor, expedition to 'Ethiopia', 20, 21, 49

Netekamani, 49; reign of, 50; name at Amara, 68; at Barkal, 73; at Meroe, 77, 81; at Wad ben Naqa, 87, 134; at Naqa, 88, 89, 90; colossal statues at Argo, 68, 101, 102, 103, 163

Noba, the, 55, 56, 57

Nobatae, the, 56

Nuri, visited by Hoskins, 27; burials at, 31; description of site, 70ff.; types of burial, 148

offering tables, 113, 152; re-used, 85

Philae, temple at, 50, 52

physical appearance, 154ff.

Piankhy, 31; pyramid at Kurru, 71, 86

Pliny, cited, 20, 21, 47, 49

pottery, 114; classification, 117; from cemeteries at Meroe, 85; Christian period sherds in W. Africa, 166

priests, ritual murder by, 16; at Jebel Barkal, 29; role in society, 153

Psammetichus II, 15, 32, 74, 161

pyramids, method of building, 86

Quili, Jebel, description of site, 96

Qostol, 56

Red Sea, trade routes, 34

Reisner, G. A., excavations, 27; chronology, 31, 35, 42

reliefs in chapels and temples, 106ff.; on Sun Temple, Meroe, 108
religion, 141ff.
'Roman bath' (Meroe), 79; statues from, 103

Sakhmak, 73
sculpture, 101; Argo colossi, 101; Musawwarat, 102; Naqa, 102; Temple of Iris, 102; statues from 'Roman bath', 103; lions from Meroe and Basa, 103
sculptured reliefs, 105ff.
Sebewyemeker, 143, 144
Sebua, Wadi es-, 63
Semna, 67
Seneca, cited, 21
Sennar, 62; southernmost site, 97
Senkamanisken, 74
Shablul, 63
Shanakdakhete, first Meroitic inscription, 91, 134
Sherkarer, 50, 68; at Qeili, 96, 163
silver, jewellery, 125; lamps, 127; cup, 129
skeletal material, 154
Soba (Alwa), 57, 97
Sotades, 122
Strabo, cited, 18, 44
Sun Temple (Meroe), 81
Syene (Aswan), 13, 18, 22

Taharqa, 31; building at Kawa, 69; burial at Nuri, 70, 72; building at

Napata, 73, 74; physical appearance, 154
Takideamani, 128
Tanqasi, burials at, 56, 57
Tanwetamani, 31, 70, 74
Tanyidamani, 42, 43; at Barkal, 73; relief from Meroe, 105
Tarekeniwal, 134
Teqerideamani, 35, 49, 52; in Lion Temple, Meroe, 84
Teriteqas, 42, 43; at Meroe, 81; stela, 84
thumb rings, 110
tools, 162
Toshka, 64
Trigger, B., cited, 133
Tuthmosis IV, at Barkal, 74

Umm Usuda, 95, 145
Ushara burials, 56

Wainwright, G.A., cited, 32, 38
weapons, 162
Woolley, C.L., excavations at Areika and Karanog, 28
writing, 132, 133ff.; correlation of Egyptain and Meroitic hieroglyphs, 134; and with Meroitic cursive, 136

X-Group people, 56, 126, 162

Yoruba, the, 167

Zyhlarz, E., cited, 133

COLLEGE WITHDRAWN THOMAS LIBRARY
ST. PAUL, MINNESOTA
UST
Libraries